KNOYDART

TO

MORVERN

KNOYDART
TO MORVERN

A personal survey of the glens from Knoydart to Morvern for mountainbikers and walkers

by

Peter D. Koch-Osborne

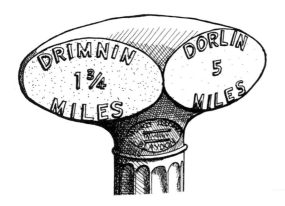

CICERONE PRESS
MILNTHORPE CUMBRIA ENGLAND

ISBN 1 85284 282 2

British Library Cataloguing-in-Publication Data.
A catalogue record for this book is
available from the British Library.

Then I'll hit the trail for that promising land;
Go mad in good company,
        find a good country,
Make a clean sweep or make a clean end.
            C. Day Lewis
            The Magnetic Mountain.
            (Penguin Dictionary of
                Modern Quotations)

Cover pictures :- Glen Kingie

            on the Barrisdale path

Index

Quoich to Knoydart   14
Quoich to Knoydart Routes   18
Glen More & Gleann Beag   22
Glen Arnisdale   24
Glen Quoich   27
Loch Loyne   30
Glen Kingie   34
Glen Barrisdale   38
Gleann na Guiserein   41
Gleann an Dubh-Lochain   44

Morar and Lochaber   46
Morar and Lochaber Routes   50
Loch Garry   55
Gleann Cia-aig   58
Glen Mallie   62
Glen Dessarry   65
Glen Pean   68
Gleann Suileag   71
Gleann Fionnlighe   75
Gleann Dubh Lighe   77
Glen Finnan   78
Borrodale Burn   80
Glen Tarbet   82

Ardnamurchan to Ardgour   84
A'murchan to A'gour Routes   88
Rubha Aird   91
Loch Shiel   94
Glen Hurich   97
Glen Scaddle   100
Cona Glen   104

Morvern   108
Morvern Routes   112
Glen Cripesdale   115
Auliston Point   119
Gleann Dubh   122
Loch Teacuis   126
Savary Glen   128

Link Routes   132

Introduction

Access to the tracks on the following pages can rarely be regarded as an absolute right by the cyclist or walker. Almost all land is private and it is often only the good nature of the owners that allows us to travel unhindered over the land. In Scottish law the term trespass implies nuisance or damage. In practice sensible conduct removes any possibility of nuisance. Respect the grouse season (12th August to 10th December) and deer stalking (stags: 1 July to 20th October, and hinds: 21st October to 15th February). Your author has not once met with any animosity in meeting gamekeepers. Only good conduct will ensure continued access. Cyclists - stay on the trail and slow down!

Conservation of the wild areas of Scotland is of paramount importance. Users of this guide must appreciate that the very ground over which you walk or cycle will be damaged if care is not taken. Please do not use a bike on soft peat paths and tread carefully on other than a stony track. Many of the tracks are themselves an eyesore. So-called development can cause irreparable damage. Make sure, as walkers and cyclists we encourage the conservation of our wilderness areas without the pressure of our activities causing further damage. In publishing this book great responsibility is placed on you, the reader, to respect the needs of the region. If all you need is exercise - go to a sports centre! If you appreciate the unique qualities of these wild places they are yours to enjoy - with care! Careless conduct not only damages what we seek to enjoy, but equally seriously gives landowners good reason to restrict access.

<u>The Maps</u> on the following pages provide sufficient detail for exploration of the glens but the O.S. Landranger maps of the region should also be used if the geographical context of the area is to be fully appreciated. These maps, and the knowledge of their proper use are essential if a longer tour or cross country route is to be undertaken.

<u>The mountain bike</u> has in your author's opinion been badly named. It does not belong on the high tops but is ideal in the glens covering about twice the distance of the average walker, quietly. It allows full appreciation of the surroundings and makes possible further exploration into the wilderness especially on short winter days. The bike must be a well maintained machine complete with a few essential spares as a broken bike miles from anywhere can be serious. Spare gear is best carried in a light rucksack or in good quality panniers. Front panniers help distribute weight and prevent 'wheelies'. Heavy rucksacks upset balance, cause backache, and put more weight onto one's already battered posterior! The brightly coloured 'high profile' image of mountainbiking, hyped up by glossy magazines is, in your author's opinion, unsuited to the remote glens. These wild areas are sacred and deserve a more inconspicuous approach.

<u>Clothing</u>. for the off-road cyclist is an important consideration. Traditional road cycling gear is unsuitable. High ankle trainers are best in summer and lightweight summer walking boots are best for winter cycling. A variety of thin or fleece 'longs' with a thermal inner layer keep legs warm in any season, even shorts have been seen in July! A man-made thermal 'top' or T-shirt with

one, (or two in winter) fleece zip jackets will keep your trunk warm. Avoid cotton at all costs - it is too absorbent. The wearing of a helmet is personal choice - a definite 'yes' if road cycling - freedom versus safety off-road. It depends how and where you ride. In any event a helmet cover and head-band will be needed in winter - or a baladava - also good ski gloves. Protection against exposure should be as for mountain walking. Remember many glens are as high as English hilltops. Also include full water-proofs in your pack.

Clothing for the walker in the glens is much as above, substituting the 'skid lid' for heavier boots and possibly gaiters. An extra layer, or heavier waterproof jacket should be taken for the higher passes and if mountain summits are to be included. In winter, conditions above (and sometimes in) the glens necessitate specialized gear and experience - beyond the scope of this book.

Safety and conduct are two important considerations. Never be without a good map, this book (!), a whistle (and knowledge of its proper use), compass, emergency rations, and spare clothing. Word of your planned route should be left together with your estimated time of arrival. The bothies must be left tidy - with firewood where appropriate- for the next visitor. Don't be too proud to remove someone else's litter. It should not be necessary to repeat the Country Code and the Mountain Bike Code. The true lover of the wild places needs peace and space - not rules and regulations. With common sense and manners there is room for the walker, cyclist and landowner!

River crossings are a major consideration when planning long through routes in wild regions of Scotland. It must be remembered that snowmelt from the high mountains can turn what is a fordable burn in early morning into a raging torrent by mid afternoon. Walkers should hold on to each other, taking turns to move. Rivers can be easier to cross with a bike, as the bike can be moved, brakes applied, and used to assist balance as feet are moved. The procedure is to remove boots and socks, replace boots only, make sure you can't drop anything and cross – ouch !! Drain boots well, dry your feet, and the theory is that your still dry socks will help to warm your feet up. Snowmelt is cold enough to hurt. Choose a wide shallow place to cross and above all don't take risks.

Ascents on a bike should be tackled slowly in a very low gear, sitting down to help the rear wheel grip. Bar end extensions help. Standing on the pedals causes wheel slip, erosion of the track and is tiring. Pushing a bike, especially if laden, is no fun and often the result of starting the climb too fast, in the wrong gear, standing up, or all three!

Descents on a bike can be exhilarating, but a fast descent is hard on both bike and rider, and can be dangerous (see 'helmets'!). If your rear wheel is locked this causes erosion. It is also ill-mannered (at best) towards others to ride too fast.

Last but not least I make no apology for repeating my request for good manners. We walk and cycle in what is a working environment, however wild or desolate it may sometimes appear. Smile and be pleasant - the guy you meet may own the entire view!

The Maps

The maps are drawn to depict the features most relevant to the explorer of the glens. North is at the top of each map and all maps, apart from introductory section maps and detail maps, are to the same scale :- 1km or 0.6miles being shown on each map. An attempt has been made to present the maps in a pictorially interesting way. A brief explanation of the various features is set out below:-

Tracks:-

One of the prime objects of these books is to grade the tracks according to roughness. This information is essential to the cyclist and useful to the walker. With due respect to the O.S. one "other road, drive or track" can take twice as long to cycle as another, yet both may be depicted in the same way. Your author's method of grading is set out below:-

metalled road. Not too many fortunately, public roads are generally included only to locate the start of a route.

good track, hardly rutted, nearly as fast as a road to cycle on but can be tedious to walk far on. Most are forest tracks.

the usual rutted estate track, rough but all rideable on a mountain bike. Not too tedious to walk on.

rough, very rutted track, nearly all rideable. Either very stony or boggy or overgrown. Can be rough even to walk.

walker's path. Only part rideable but not usually advised with a bike. May be used as part of a through bike route.

10

<u>Relief</u> is depicted in two ways. The heavy lines depict main mountain ridges, summits and spurs thus :-

Contour lines are also used, at 50m intervals, up to about 600m. This adds shape to the glens as mapped and gives an idea of how much climbing is involved. Reference to gradient profiles at the start of each section compares the various routes.

<u>Crags</u> are shown thus :- with major areas of scree dotted.

<u>Rivers</u> generally 'uncrossable' are shown as two lines whilst small streams or burns are shown using a single line. Note, great care is needed crossing larger burns and rivers. Falling in can cause embarrassment at best, exposure or even drowning at worst. Please don't take risks - besides, you'd get this book wet!!

loch or lochan

<u>Buildings</u> and significant ruins are shown as :......

<u>Bridges</u> are rather obviously shown thus :- ✕ with an indication of type of construction to assist location.

<u>Trees</u> are so numerous your author wishes there were an easier way of drawing them but there isn't!! etc...

11

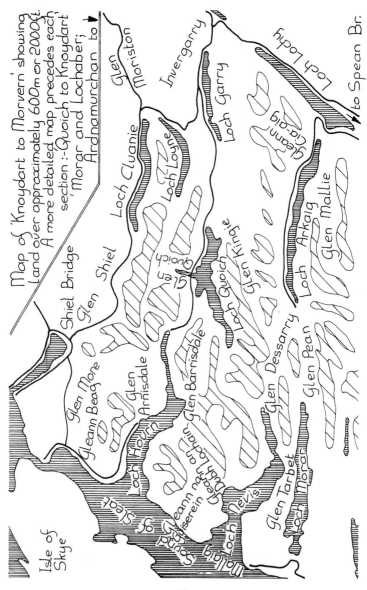

Map of 'Knoydart to Morven' showing land over approximately 600m or 2000ft. A more detailed map precedes each section :- Quoich to Knoydart; Morar and Lochaber; Ardnamurchan to

to Spean Br.

Loch Lochy
Invergarry
Glen Moriston
Glen Garry
Gleann Cia-aig
Glen Mallie
Loch Arkaig
Loch Cluanie
Loch Loyne
Loch Quoich
Glen Kingie
Glen Dessarry
Glen Pean
Loch 75 uca Quoich
Shiel Bridge
Glen Shiel
Glen More
Gleann Beag
Glen Arnisdale
Loch Hourn
Glen Barrisdale
Gleann an Dubh Lochain
Glen Tarbet
Loch Morar
Loch Nevis
Glen
Loch Arkaig

Isle of Skye

Kyle of Sleat

Mallaig

12

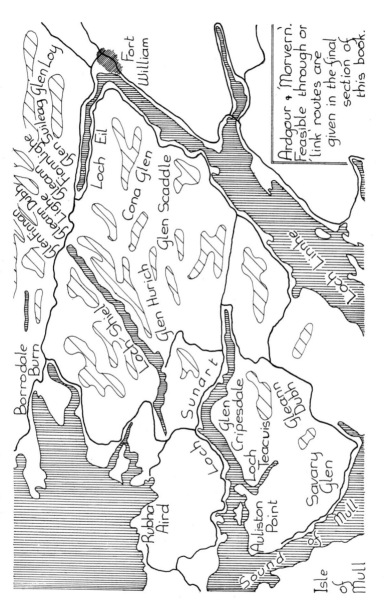

Glen Loy

Glen Suileag

Gleann Suileag

Ligeir

Gleann Dubh

Glenfinnan

Borrodale Burn

Loch Eil

Cona Glen

Glen Scaddle

Glen Hurich

Loch Shiel

Fort William

Ardgour & 'Morvern'.
Feasible through or
'link' routes are
given in the final
section of this book.

Loch Linnhe

Loch Sunart

Rubha Aird

Glen Cripesdale

Loch Teacuis

Gleann Dubh

Auliston Point

Savary Glen

Sound of Mull

Isle of Mull

13

Quoich to Knoydart

Glen More & Gleann Beag 22
Glen Arnisdale 24
Glen Quoich 27
Loch Loyne 30
Glen Kingie 34
Glen Barrisdale 38
Gleann na Guiserein 41
Gleann an Dubh-Lochain 44

Quoich to Knoydart

Access:- This exciting region lies south of the Kyle of Lochalsh to Invergarry road; Glen Shiel, Loch Cluanie and Glen Garry. Two minor roads penetrate the wilds. Firstly, over the tortuous Mam Ratagan pass, the Glenelg road, once the main route to Skye, thrusts west and curls around the coast to Arnisdale. Secondly, the Tomdoun road heads west to Kinloch Hourn. Access to Knoydart is either by boat from Mallaig, or on foot from Kinloch Hourn, Strathan or Glenfinnan. Also, a boat runs from Arnisdale by arrangement. The attraction of the region is its inaccessibility.

Accommodation:- Hotels at Cluanie and Tomdoun, B&B's at Arnisdale and Glen Shiel, and a youth hostel particularly well situated at Ratagan. Camping at Glen Shiel and Glen Garry. More information on accommodation at Inverie on page 41. There is camping and a (busy) bothy at Barrisdale.

Geographical Features:- A wild mountain area with generally little soil cover, always providing a challenge to man's efforts. The region became over populated only to suffer badly in the Highland Clearances. Communications have always limited development, this being to the lover of wild places, the main attraction. This difficult access has kept mass afforestation at bay in much of the region.

Mountains:- Where to begin? Knoydart proudly boasts three fine Munros, and many lesser peaks. Ladhar Bheinn, Luinne Bheinn and Meall Buidhe are fine, remote mountains indeed. Together with Sgurr na Ciche on the Loch Nevis/Loch Quoich divide (the most shapely peak in the area) these represent some of the finest mountains on the Scottish mainland. These "stars" are however in good company. Beinn Sgritheall stands, indeed towers, over Arnisdale and notable peaks lie all around Loch Quoich - then of course there is the South Kintail Ridge..... what an area!!

Rivers:- Generally rivers in this region are short and subject to sudden rise due to the high rainfall. For example the considerable River Shiel is only 15km or about 10 miles long. Most of the rivers can be impossible or dangerous to cross within three miles of their source - take particular note of the bridges.

Forests:- The largest is the Mam Ratagan Forest which clothes both sides of the pass. Further planted forests punctuate the Arnisdale road. Apart from Gleann na Guiserein on Knoydart inaccessibility limits forestry although tree planting is advancing up Glen Kingie. The weather and deer limit natural woods to steep, but sheltered hillsides.

Lochs:- Loch Quoich, with its scarred shoreline and flooded, bridged offshoot will always look like a reservoir however one tries to imagine it isn't. Loch Loyne likewise, inconsiderately flooding the old road. So too Loch Cluanie. The sea-lochs are more exciting; Loch Alsh, Loch Duich and the straits of Kyle Rhea wrap themselves around the Arnisdale peninsula while dark Loch Hourn and the more open Loch Nevis encircle Knoydart.

Emergency:- The entire region comprises remote glens, high mountains and difficult access. Kinloch Hourn, Strathan and, of course Inverie are populated, there is a 'keeper at Barrisdale. Beyond that you are very much on your own so plan with care, well within your abilities, and keep an eye on the weather.

Quoich to Knoydart Routes 1

Glen More & Gleann Beag

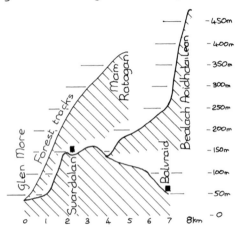

Glen Arnisdale

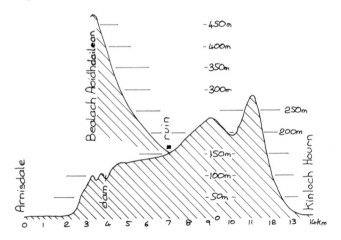

18

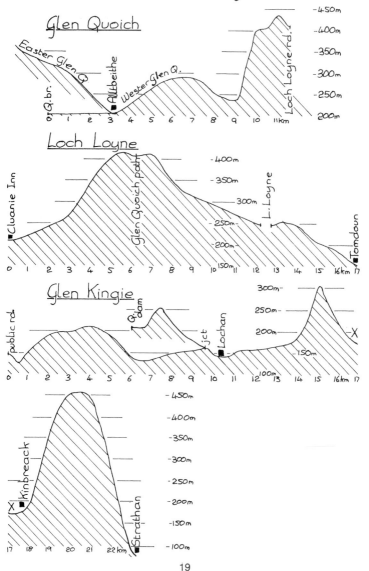

Quoich to Knoydart Routes 3

Glen Barrisdale

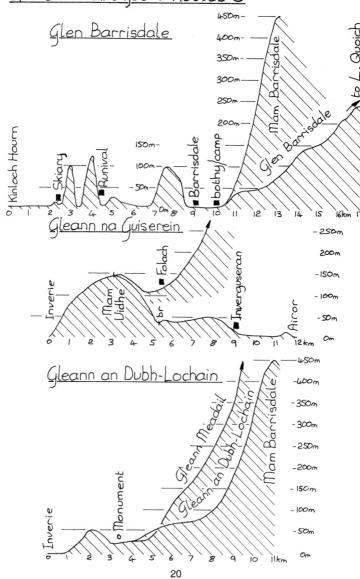

Gleann na Guiserein

Gleann an Dubh-Lochain

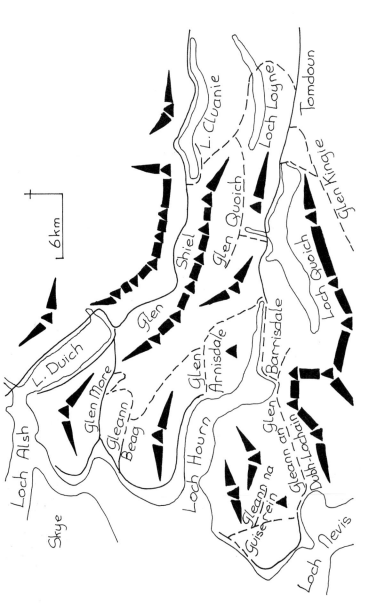

Loch Alsh

Skye

L. Duich

Loch Hourn

Loch Nevis

Glen More

Gleann Beag

Glen Shiel

Glen Arnisdale

Gleann na Guiserein

Gleann an Dubh-Lochain

Glen Barrisdale

Glen Quoich

Loch Quoich

L. Cluanie

Loch Loyne

Tomdoun

Glen Kingie

6km

Glen More & Gleann Beag 1

This 'pair' of glens may be explored on foot from one to the other (requiring transport at each end); as a cyclists 'circuit' via the public roads and Glen- elg (best done anti-clockwise as most of the rough path section is then downhill). Alternatively, the forest tracks may be explored from just below Bealach Ratagain, where there is space to park, or from Glen More itself. There is a bothy and therefore shelter at Suardalan - an ideal lunch-stop. A visit to Gleann Beag must allow time to explore the brochs. The full circuit via Glenelg is 21 km or 13 miles. Note the link track/path over Bealach Aoidhdailean to Gleann Dubh, Lochain on the Glen Arnisdale to Kinloch Hourn route; see Link Route 1 for this demanding circular tour.

Suardalan

22

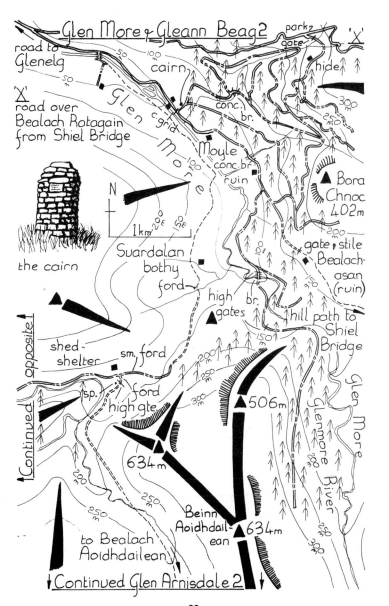

Glen More & Gleann Beag 2

park

gate

'X'

road to Glenelg

50   100

cairn

hide

300

250

'X'
road over
Bealach Rotagain
from Shiel Bridge

50

G l e n

conc. br.

c. grid

Moyle

conc. br.

ruin

N

200

300

400

1km

▲ Bora
Chnoc
402m

the cairn

200

150

gate, stile
Bealach-
asan
(ruin)

Suardalan
bothy
ford

high
gates

br.

hill path to
Shiel
Bridge

150

Continued opposite ↑

shed-
shelter

sm. ford

200

250

sp.

ford

high gte

300
m

▲ 506m

634m

Glen More

Glenmore River

200

200

300

300

250

Beinn
Aoidhdail-
ean

▲ 634m

to Bealach
Aoidhdailean

↓ Continued Glen Arnisdale 2 ↓

Glen Arnisdale 1

The rough track from Glen Arnisdale, via Gleann Dubh Lochain to Kinloch Hourn forms an important link between the ends of two public roads. Although the route is only some 14km or 9miles in length it is 113km or 70 miles by road! It is an easy, yet committing walk, or a very arduous off-road bike ride – rough, with much steep climbing. Note the link to Glen More and Gleann Beag – equally arduous with a bike; (not necessarily on a bike!). It is possible to "cheat". The Post Office at Arnisdale runs a ferry service, on demand, to Kinloch Hourn, and will carry bikes – a useful service for the road touring cyclist. Rough shelter (very rough!) can be found in the boathouses. There is a tea room at Kinloch Hourn (summer only). Refer to Link Route 1 – but only if you are fit enough!!

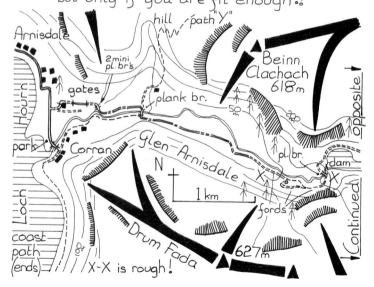

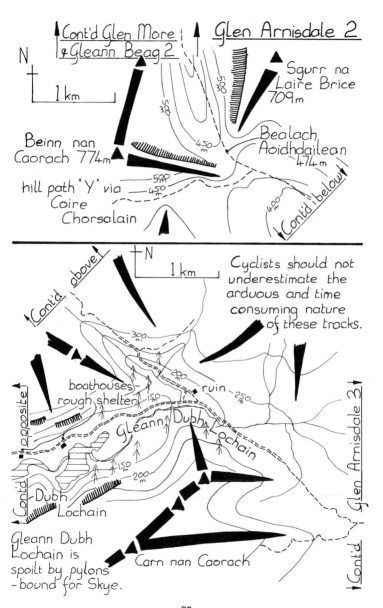

N

1 km

Sgurr na Laire Brice 709 m

Beinn nan Caorach 774 m

Bealach Aoidhdailean 474 m

hill path "Y" via Coire Chorsalain

Cont'd below

N

1 km

Cyclists should not underestimate the arduous and time consuming nature of these tracks.

Cont'd above

Cont'd opposite

boathouses- rough shelter

ruin

Gleann Dubh Lochain

Cont'd -Dubh Lochain

Gleann Dubh Lochain is spoilt by pylons -bound for Skye.

Carn nan Caorach

Glen Arnisdale 3

Cont'd

25

Glen Arnisdale 3

Kinloch Hourn

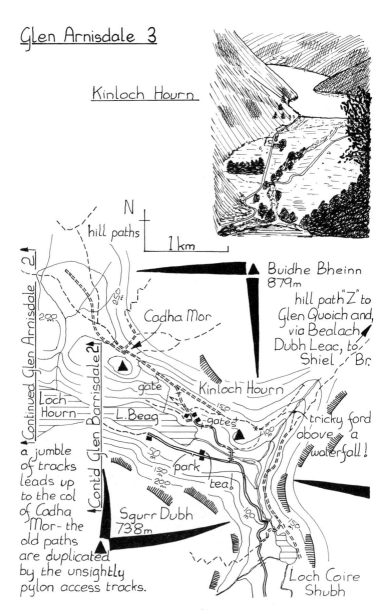

N

1 km

hill paths

Continued Glen Arnisdale (2)

Loch Hourn

a jumble of tracks leads up to the col of Cadha Mor- the old paths are duplicated by the unsightly pylon access tracks.

Contd Glen Barrisdale (2)

Buidhe Bheinn 879m

hill path"Z" to Glen Quoich and, via Bealach Dubh Leac, to Shiel Br.

Cadha Mor

250

200

gate

Kinloch Hourn

L. Beag

gates

150

tricky ford above a waterfall!

100

50

park

tea!

150

200

Sgurr Dubh 738m

100

150

Loch Coire Shubh

Glen Quoich 1

The Glen Quoich track starts from the western end of the Loch Quoich bridge and runs north to Alltbeithe. From here a track, quickly degenerating into a path runs north west over Bealach Duibh Leac to Glen Shiel, picking up the Kinloch Hourn path on its way. The main track however runs east from Alltbeithe and is cycleable as far as the ruin some 8km or 5miles from the start. From here a footpath continues, soon climbing to the left (north east) to join the old Cluanie Inn to Tomdoun road - refer to Loch Loyne. This section is just about passable with - but not on - a bike if starting from the Inn and tackling the roughest section downhill, thereby avoiding the dodgy bridge in (yes, in!) Loch Loyne. Refer Link Route 1 . There is no shelter in Glen Quoich.

Loch Quoich Bridge

27

Glen Quoich 2

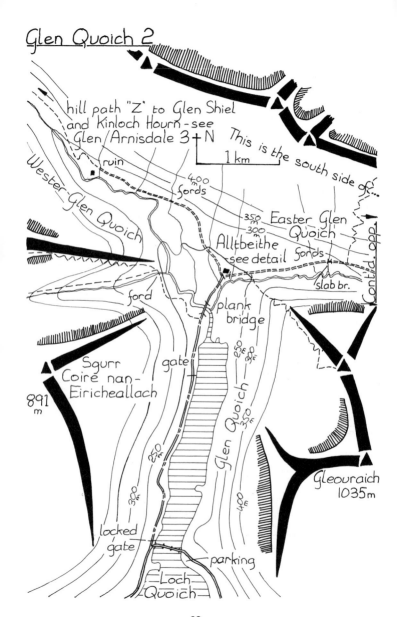

hill path "Z" to Glen Shiel
and Kinloch Hourn - see
Glen/Arnisdale 3 + N

This is the south side of...

1 km

ruin

Wester Glen Quoich

400m
fords

350m
300m

Easter Glen Quoich

Alltbeithe
see detail

fords

slab br.

contd. opp.

ford

plank
bridge

250m
300m

gate

Sgurr
Coire nan-
Eiricheallach

891 m

Glen Quoich

350m

250m

400m

300m

Gleouraich
1035m

locked
gate

parking

Loch
Quoich

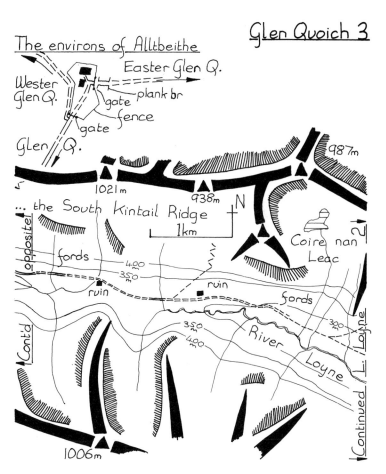

The environs of Alltbeithe

Easter Glen Q.

Wester Glen Q.

plank br

gate

fence

gate

Glen Q.

987m

1021m

938m

the South Kintail Ridge

N

1km

opposite

Contd

fords

400

350m

ruin

ruin

fords

Coire nan Leac

300

2

Continued L. Loyne

350

400

River

Loyne

1006m

ruin – Quoich-Loyne watershed

Loch Loyne 1

The Loch Loyne road was once the public road from Cluanie Inn to Tomdoun, indeed it is metalled, although the surface is now (1998) starting to disintegrate. This road became an estate road when Loch Loyne was dammed and a 700 metre section of road and two bridges were submerged. However, Loch Loyne is regularly well below its high "tide" mark revealing the flooded section and its bridges. Unfortunately one of the bridges is in dangerous condition (it may not even be there) so your author cannot

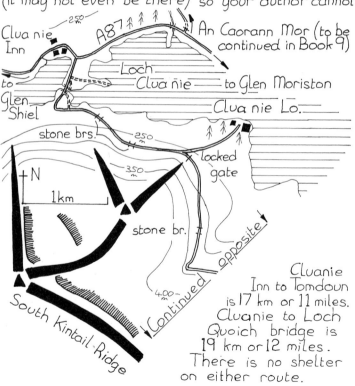

Cluanie Inn

A87   An Caorann Mor (to be continued in Book 9)

250 m

Loch Cluanie — to Glen Moriston

to Glen Shiel

Cluanie Lo.

stone brs.   250 m

locked gate

+N

1km

350 m

stone br.

Continued opposite

400 m

South Kintail Ridge

Cluanie Inn to Tomdoun is 17 km or 11 miles. Cluanie to Loch Quoich bridge is 19 km or 12 miles. There is no shelter on either route.

30

recommend using this crossing point. Landing in a deep, fast flowing channel accompanied by several tonnes of masonry would be more than a little uncomfortable! Alternatives lie via Glen Quoich (rough for bikes - take section X-X -below- downhill), and via the forest tracks to the road above Loch Loyne. Note that exploring the old road from Cluanie, and separately from Tomdoun, is worthwhile in two halves; a slightly sad piece of our Highland transport heritage.

Loch C.

Creag a Mhaim 947m

stone bridge

stone bridges

ruins

ends

River Loyne

1km

↖ Continued opposite

Continued Glen Quoich 31 →

← Continued Glen Quoich

Continued Loch Loyne 3 →

Continued Loch Loyne 3 →

Loch Loyne 3

Loch Loyne
-flooded road when loch is full.

Typical low-water condition -the north bridge is unsafe - south bridge Ok '97!

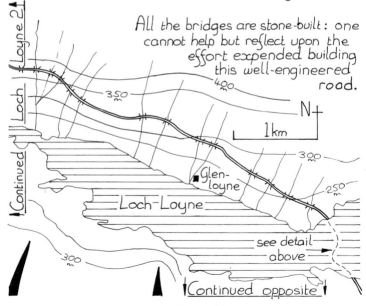

All the bridges are stone-built: one cannot help but reflect upon the effort expended building this well-engineered road.

Continued Loch Loyne 2

350 m

400

N

1 km

Glen-loyne

Loch-Loyne

300 m

250 m

see detail above

300 m

Continued opposite

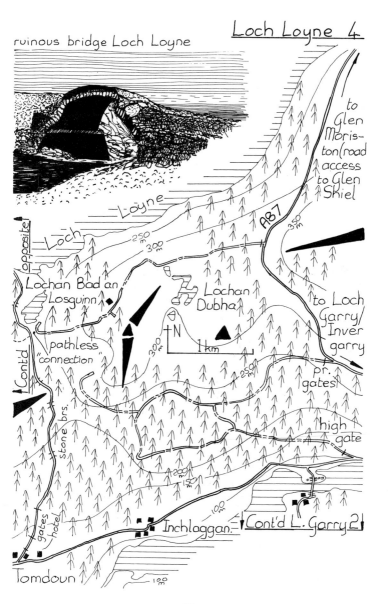

Loch Loyne 4

ruinous bridge Loch Loyne

to Glen Moriston(road access to Glen Shiel

Loyne

A87

350m

Loch

opposite

250m
300m

Lochan Bad an Losguinn

Lochan Dubha

to Loch Garry/ Inver garry

+N

300m

1km

pathless "connection"

250m

pr. gates

Cont'd

stone brs.

high gate

100m
150m

gates

hotel

100m

Inchlaggan

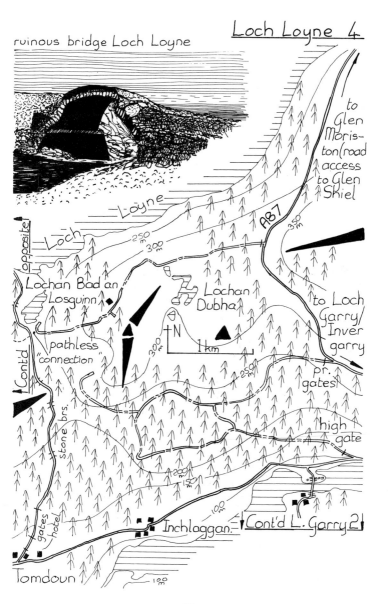Cont'd L. Garry 2

Tomdoun

100m

33

Glen Kingie 1

This route starts on Glen Kingie 4. This map depicts the higher reaches of the glen. The hill path provides access to the remote mountains between Loch Quoich and Glen Kingie. This is walkers' country - a bike would damage the paths and, simply, be out of place here.

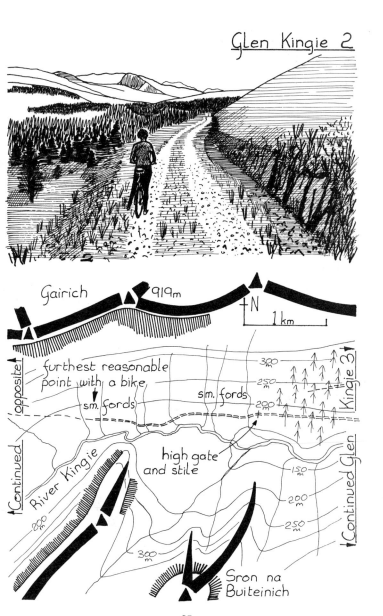

Gairich

919m

N

1 km

furthest reasonable
point with a bike,
sm. fords

sm. fords

300 m

250 m

200 m

Continued Glen Kingie 3

opposite

high gate
and stile

River Kingie

150 m

200 m

250 m

Continued Glen

200 m

300 m

Sron na
Buiteinich

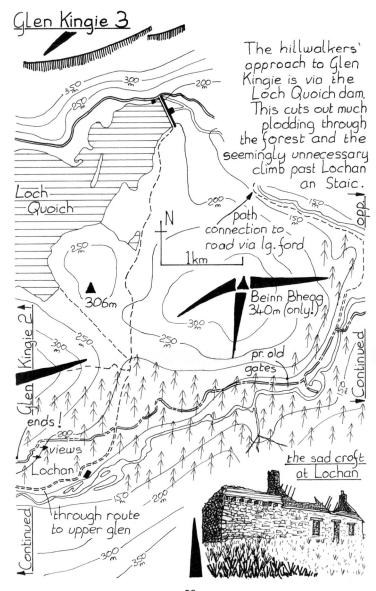

The hillwalkers' approach to Glen Kingie is via the Loch Quoich dam. This cuts out much plodding through the forest and the seemingly unnecessary climb past Lochan an Staic.

350m
300m
250m
200m

Loch Quoich

200m

150m
150m
opp.

path connection to road via lg. ford

N

1km

250m

▲ 306m

300m

Beinn Bheag 340m (only!)

Glen Kingie 2 ←

250m
300m
250m

pr. old gates

150m

Continued →

Glen Kingie ends!

views Lochan

200m

150m
200m

← Continued

through route to upper glen

300m
250m

the sad croft at Lochan

The Glen Kingie track starts by **descending** from the public road about 2km west of Tomdoun. The track crosses the bridge above picturesque rapids which drain Loch Poulary. Cyclists can aim for the viewpoint (G.K.3); the farthest practical point to cycle (G.K.2) or the ruins at Lochan. If heading higher up the glen be sure to take the rough track via Lochan.

Tomdoun 2km

park

Loch Poulary

Power Sta.

gates

150

N

1km

lg. ford

high gate

150m

200m

200m

boggy o'grown path to Garrygualach

The only shelter in Glen Kingie is well up the glen at Kinbreack.

Lochan an Staic

cont'd opposite

Glen Barrisdale 1

Glen Barrisdale is not a cyclists' route. The path is rough and cycling is quite reasonably discouraged. The path from Kinloch Hourn is the main approach, other than by boat, to Knoydart. Knoydart is a very special place, so please do not cycle - and explore the delights of Barrisdale on foot.

L. Hourn

pl. br.

50

200 m

Barrisdale Bay

50 m

conc. br.

Carn Mairi

Barrisdale

85

bothy camp

plank br.

569 m

150

50

100

Coir a Chearcaill

pl. br.

Glen Barrisdale

200 m

pl. br.

Continued opposite

Cont'd Dubh

Gleann an Lochain 2

450m Mam Barrisdale

665m

Gleann Unndalain

N

1km

hill path to L. Quoich

38

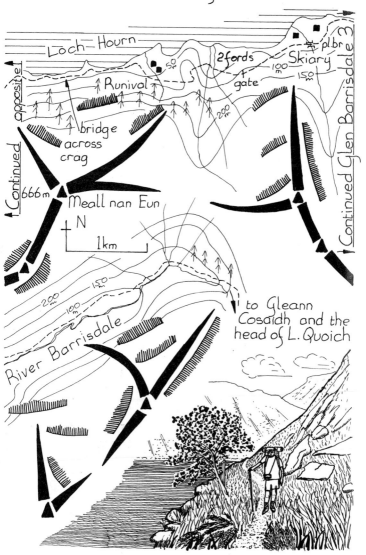

Loch Hourn

50m

2 fords

gate

Skiary

pl.br

100m

150m

200m

opposite

Runival

bridge across crag

Continued

666m

Meall nan Eun

N

1 km

Continued Glen Barrisdale 3

200m

150m

100m

River Barrisdale

to Gleann Cosaidh and the head of L. Quoich

↑ Cont'd Glen Arnisdale 3 ↑

Loch Beag

tea

100

200 m

park

250 m

+N

1km

← Contd Glen Barrisdale 2 ↑ →

↑ Contd Glen Barrisdale 2 ↑

please take note of the many signs at Kinloch Hourn.

This map depicts the start of the path to Barrisdale from Kinloch Hourn.

<u>Note:-</u>
The sketch on the previous page shows your author hard at work researching the shore of Loch Hourn. Specialized gear includes:- walking stick, floppy sunhat, shades and shorts. Rucksack includes provisions for a week to cover for a day or two off research, to scale Ladhar Bheinn. It's a tough life, but someone has to do it!! This also proves that the rain at Kinloch Hourn occasionally, just occasionally, actually stops!

Access to Gleann na Guiserein is by boat from Mallaig, or on foot from Kinloch Hourn, Glenfinnan or Strathan. The boat runs, at the time of writing, on Mondays, Wednesdays and Fridays - weather permitting. If the weather is too rough for the boat it is no good for outdoor activities either! At Inverie overnight stays can be arranged at one of two bunk-houses or B.B. There is a restaurant/tea rm. shop and a pub. Telephone in advance from Mallaig. The above arrangements are worth the effort; Knoydart is unique in its isolation. Scope for exploration on foot is limitless but a bike (which can be taken on the boat) is limited to the Gleann na Guiserein tracks and the metalled coast road. This makes a circuit of 22 km or 14 miles plus the 'leg' to Folach. The section from Airor to Inverguseran is rough and I am reliably informed that the bull is friendly, but we've not met! There is a major ford at Inverguseran - stepping stones with one displaced. A bike is handy to lean on, walkers will need a long stick or pole. Flood water makes the crossing impassable - see map for walkers' (only) route avoiding the ford (and the over-enthusiastic horse at Inverguseran!). Refer also to Gleann an Dubh Lochain, part of which may also be explored by bike.

The only shelter is in a huge cow shed just north of Airor - but you may have to share it.

Inverie

Gleann na Guiserein 2

The coast road from Inverie to Airor extends some 11km or 7miles. This is an estate road, not a public road, hence the absence of tax discs!

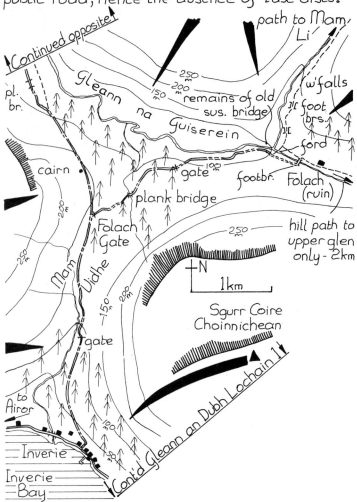

Continued opposite

path to Mam Li

w'falls

remains of old sus. bridge

foot brs.

ford

pl. br.

Gleann na Guiserein

cairn

gate

footbr.

Folach (ruin)

plank bridge

Folach Gate

hill path to upper glen only - 2km

Mam Uidhe

+N

1km

Sgurr Coire Choinnichean

gate

to Airor

Inverie

Cont'd Gleann an Dubh Lochain 1

Inverie Bay

42

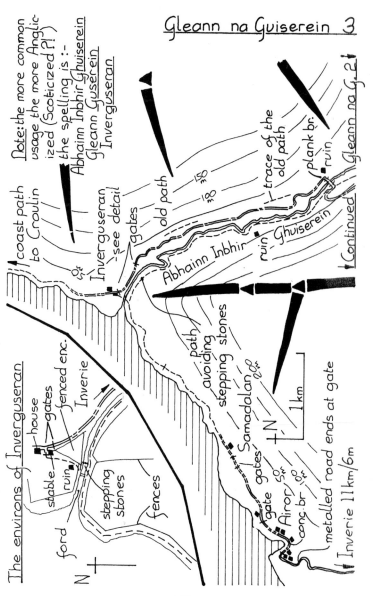

Gleann na Guiserein 3

Note: the more common usage the name Anglicized (Scoticized?!) the spelling is :-
Abhainn Inbhir Ghuiserein
Gleann Guiseran
Inverguseran

coast path to Croulin

Inverguseran - see detail

gates

old path

150 ₘ

100 ₘ

trace of the old path

plank br.
ruin

ruin Ghuiserein

Abhainn Inbhir

Continued Gleann na G.2↓

path avoiding stepping stones

Samadalan 20ₘ

1 km

+ N

metalled road ends at gate

Airor 5ₘ   10ₘ

conc. br.

Inverie 11km/6m ←

The environs of Inverguseran

house

gates

fenced enc.

Inverie

stable

ruin

ford

stepping stones

fences

+ N

43

Gleann an Dubh-Lochain 1

This glen provides an easy walk or short cycle ride out of Inverie. The head of the loch is the limit with a bike as the path, though well engineered, is wet in places and suffers from erosion. Beyond Mam Barrisdale is not cycling country either. Gleann an Dubh-Lochain links Gleann na Guiserein with Glen Barrisdale and Kinloch Hourn forming the main land access to Knoydart. The alternative is from Strathan (or indeed Glenfinnan) via Glen Dessarry and Sourlies - a two day trek. There is shelter at Torcuileainn. The distance from Inverie to the head of Loch an Dubh-Lochain is 8 km (5 miles) and to Mam Barrisdale is 11 km or 7 miles.

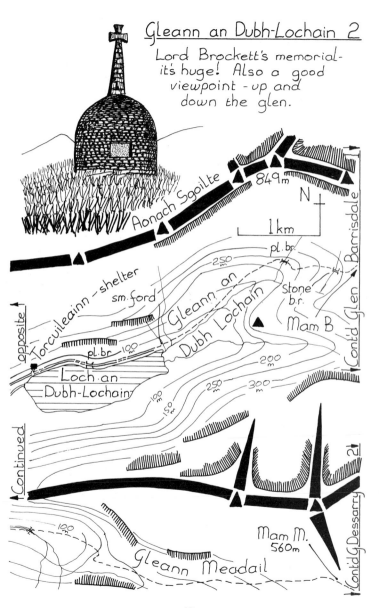

Gleann an Dubh-Lochain 2

Lord Brockett's memorial-
it's huge! Also a good
viewpoint - up and
down the glen.

Aonach Sgoilte   849m

N

1 km

Torcuileainn - shelter   sm. ford

pl. br.

Gleann an
Dubh Lochain

Stone
b.r.

Mam B

250

200 m

100

pl. br.   100

Loch an
Dubh-Lochain

150 m

250 m

300 m

opposite

Cont'd Glen Barrisdale

Continued

Mam M.
560m

21

Gleann Meadail

100

Cont'd G. Dessarry

Morar and Lochaber

Loch Garry	55
Gleann Cia-aig	58
Glen Mallie	62
Glen Dessarry	65
Glen Pean	68
Gleann Suileag	71
Gleann Fionnlighe	75
Gleann Dubh Lighe	77
Glen Finnan	78
Borrodale Burn	80
Glen Tarbet	82

Morar and Lochaber

Access:- This area lies south and east of Knoydart, north and west of the Great Glen and north of the Mallaig 'Road to the Isles'. The only other road access which begins to penetrate this remote area is the Loch Arkaig road - a tortuous single track affair ending just before Strathan. From here glens radiate giving access to everywhere from Knoydart to Loch Nevis, and Loch Morar to Glen Finnan. The railway from Fort William to Mallaig can be used to great advantage allowing a return to base from one of several possible point-to-point routes.

Accommodation:- Fort Bill has everything - usually in excess. The Mallaig road has a good supply of B.B's and campsites especially at its western end. The interior of the region has virtually no accommodation - which is indeed its attraction.

Geographical Features :- This is fjord country, the deep glens and long, deep lochs keep easy access at bay. Only the eastern end of the region, with its transport links, has any amount of forestry (with the good 'biking that provides). As in Knoydart, limited soil cover combined with difficult access keeps any population to the southern fringe of the region - along the Fort William to Mallaig road and rail route.

Mountains:- The east of the region is devoid of what your author would describe as 'proper' mountains. However, travelling west two main groups dominate the centre of the region. The Sgurr nan Coireachan to Sgurr Thuilm group lie north of Corryhully in Glen Finnan; and Glen Dessarry gives access to Sgurr nan Coireachan (yes, another one!) in the great chain of mountains between Sgurr na Ciche (which really belongs to Knoydart) and Sgurr Mor (one of the Quoich hills). Further west the hills attain lesser heights, but in contrast with those in the east, are no less rugged and rocky.

Rivers:- The nature of the land gives rise to short swift-flowing rivers. It is worthy of note that the rivers Mallie, Dessarry and Pean all flow east from sources within very few miles of Lochs Nevis and Morar, via Loch Arkaig and Loch Lochy reaching the 'west' at Fort William courtesy of the River Lochy.

Forests:- The most extensively forested area is beside Loch Garry; all other eastern glens have awkward lumps of plantation uncomfortably placed around their lower reaches. The forests of Glen Pean and Glen Dessarry however, encroach into true wild country - especially the upper forests of Dessarry. This changes the feel of these sacred wild glens. How is it possible to define the acceptability of plantations in, say, Glen Loy, and the unacceptability of the same in Glen Dessarry? How wild is wild? Only the lover of these places fully understands the distinction.

Lochs:- Loch Nevis, a sea loch and Loch Morar, a fresh water loch, provide the character of the region. Wild, bleak yet beautiful stretches of water. Loch Arkaig with its tortuous road and inaccessible south shore maintains this theme in the east of this region whilst Loch Garry, comparatively tame by comparison is almost surrounded by road or track.

Emergency:- The shorter routes pose no threat, all are a quick bike ride or short walk back to the main road and civilisation. The interior of the area is altogether a more serious place, with no telephone or guaranteed occupancy even at Strathan. Always leave word when venturing into the remote glens.

Morar and Lochaber Routes 1

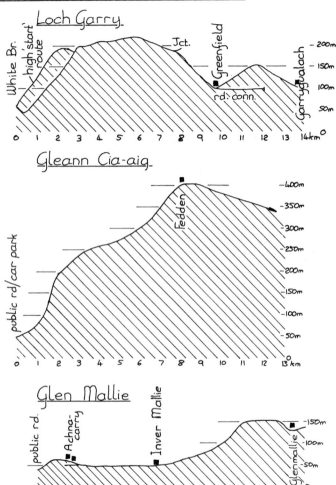

Loch Garry

White Br. · 'high start' route · Jct. · Greenfield · rd. conn. · Garrygualach

200m — 150m — 100m — 50m

0 1 2 3 4 5 6 7 8 9 10 11 12 13 14km 0

Gleann Cia-aig

public rd/car park · Fedden

400m — 350m — 300m — 250m — 200m — 150m — 100m — 50m

0 1 2 3 4 5 6 7 8 9 10 11 12 13 km 0

Glen Mallie

public rd. · Achna-carry · Inver Mallie · Glenmallie

150m — 100m — 50m

0 1 2 3 4 5 6 7 8 9 10 11 12km 0

Glen Dessarry

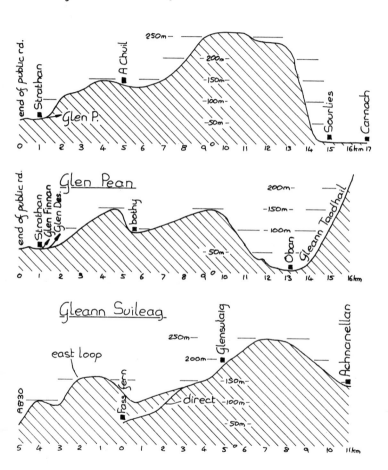

Glen Pean

Gleann Suileag

Morar and Lochaber Routes 3

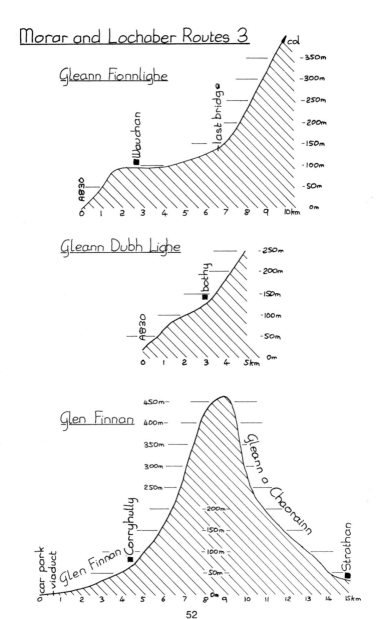

Gleann Fionnlighe

Gleann Dubh Lighe

Glen Finnan

Borrodale Burn

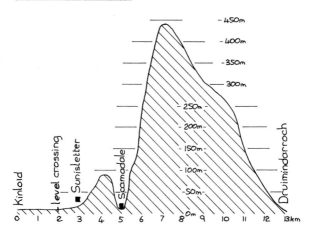

Glen Tarbet

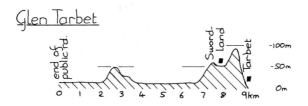

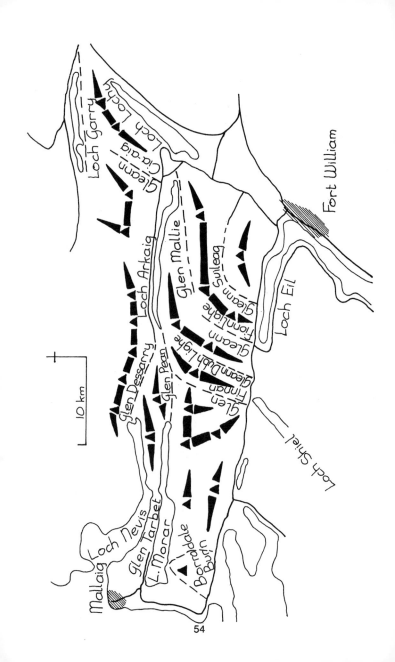

54

Loch Garry 1

After a hilly start from the White Bridge car park the Loch Garry tracks provide some excellent cycling. These tracks may be followed all the way to the Loch Garry bridge or to the rough track leading to Garryqualach, from which a rough, wet and partly overgrown walkers' path provides a tenuous connection to Glen Kingie. Beware of dead-end tracks - there are plenty of them. Track 'X', below, provides a more interesting start and the climb past Glenluie a more interesting finish. There is shelter at the Allt Ladaich crossing and at Garryqualach. Total one-way distance from White Bridge to Garryqualach is about 14 km or 9 miles, and from White Bridge to the Loch Garry bridge (Tomdoun road) is 12 km or 8 miles.

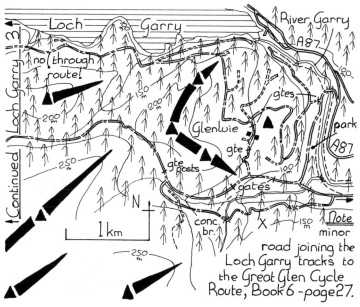

Loch ···· Garry

River Garry

A87

Continued Loch Garry 3

no through route!

200 m

250 m

150 m

200 m

Glenluie

gtes

park

A87

gte

gte posts

100 m

gates

N

1 km

conc. br.

X

150 m

250 m

Note minor road joining the Loch Garry tracks to the Great Glen Cycle Route, Book 6 - page 27.

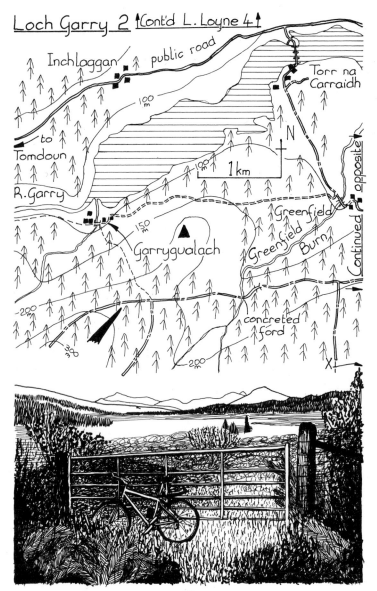

Inchlaggan

public road

100 m

to Tomdoun

R.Garry

Torr na Carraidh

N

1 km

100 m

150 m

Garrygualach

Greenfield

Greenfield Burn

← opposite →

Continued

-200 m

300

concreted ford

200

X

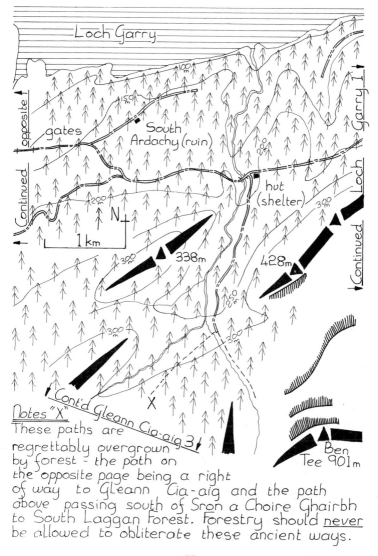

Loch Garry

100 m

150 m

opposite ◄

gates

South Ardachy (ruin)

Continued

200 m

250 m

hut (shelter)

300 m

N

1 km

300 m

338 m

428 m

Loch Garry 1

Continued ►

250 m

300 m

300 m

300 m

X

Cont'd Gleann Cia-aig 3 ►

Ben Tee 901m

Notes "X"
These paths are regrettably overgrown by forest – the path on the opposite page being a right of way to Gleann Cia-aig and the path above passing south of Sron a Choire Ghairbh to South Laggan forest. Forestry should <u>never</u> be allowed to obliterate these ancient ways.

Gleann Cia-aig 1

Gleann Cia-aig is another example of old rights of way becoming swamped by trees, this time at the northern, Loch Garry end. The lower reaches of this narrow glen are, however picturesque, and the forlorn ruin at Fedden provides a point to head for. The glen gives access to the Loch Lochy hills, a compact mountain group including the prominent Ben Tee and two Munros, Sron a Choire Ghairbh and Meall na Teanga. A further, unconnected path runs from the South Laggan Forest to the Loch Garry forests on the east side of the upper reaches of Abhainn Chia-aig. The route is only suitable for bikes within the forested area; from the forest limit proceed on foot. Note the view south from the viewpoint just above the start. The descent by bike is superb but beware walkers enjoying the forest in the vicinity of the falls and car park. Total distance from the car park (one way) to the limit of the wood is 6km or 4 miles; to Fedden is 9km or 6 miles; and to the start of the Glen Garry forest is 11·5km or 7·5 miles. Cyclists are obliged to start a little way down the road east of the car park. Walkers can take a short cut by the falls reducing the above distances by 1·5km or one mile. There is no shelter.

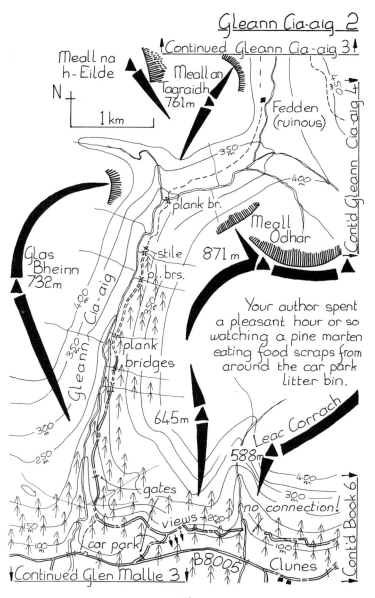

Continued Gleann Cia-aig 3

Meall na h-Eilde

Meall an Tagraidh 761m

N

1 km

Fedden (ruinous)

Cont'd Gleann Cia-aig 4

350

400

plank br.

Meall Odhar

stile

871 m

pl. brs.

Glas Bheinn 732m

Gleann Cia-aig

400

350

plank bridges

300

250

645m

Your author spent a pleasant hour or so watching a pine marten eating food scraps from around the car park litter bin.

Leac Corrach

588m

400 m

gates

no connection!

300 m

views

400

Cont'd Book 6

150 m

100 m

car park

100 m

B8005

Clunes

Continued Glen Mallie 3

59

Gleann Cia-aig 3

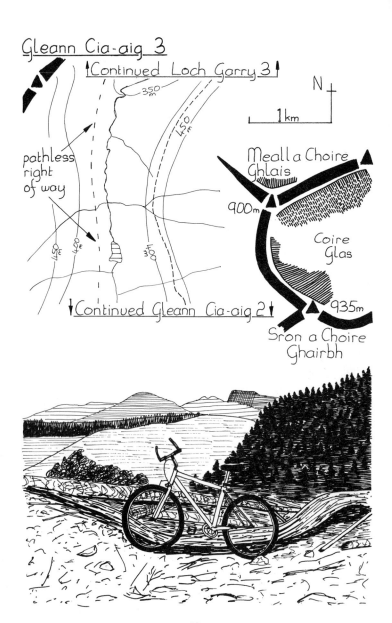

↑ Continued Loch Garry 3 ↑

N

1 km

350 m

450 m

pathless right of way

350 m

400 m

300 m

Meall a Choire Ghlais

900 m

Coire Glas

↓ Continued Gleann Cia-aig 2 ↓

935 m

Sron a Choire Ghairbh

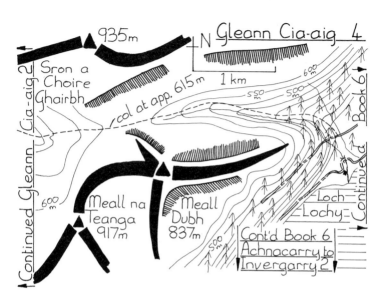

△ 935m

N

Sron a Choire Ghairbh

1 km

col at app. 615m

600 m

550 m

500 m

Continued Gleann Cia-aig 2

Continued Book 6

Meall na Teanga 917m

Meall Dubh 837m

600 m

Loch Lochy

500 m

Cont'd Book 6
Achnacarry to
Invergarry 2

Eas Chia-aig

Glen Mallie 1

The River Mallie flows almost due east into Loch Arkaig, flanked by smooth-sided hills of little note – until the upper reaches of the glen at least. The glen provides an easy bike ride with little ascent, up to the ruin, beyond which a deteriorating path leads further up the glen. There is a bothy, and therefore shelter at Invermallie; this clearly suffers over-use resulting from its size and proximity to the public road. Sadly its use, as indicated in the bothy book on your author's last visit, had nothing to do with enjoying the hills and glens. Access to the glen track is either via the outflow from Loch Arkaig (10 km or 6·5 miles to the ruin), or via Achnacarry, adding 2 km or about a mile. _Note:-_ The B8005 from Gairlochy to Clunes is part of the Great Glen Cycle route – see book 6 pages 23, 24.

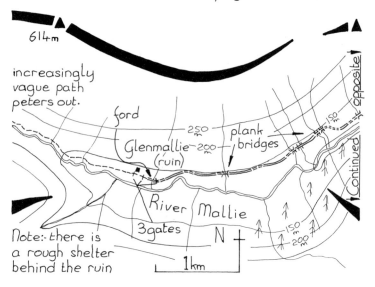

614m

increasingly
vague path
peters out.

ford

250 m — plank bridges

Glenmallie – 200 m
(ruin)

River Mallie

3 gates

N

150 m
200 m

Continued it opposite

Note:- there is
a rough shelter
behind the ruin

1 km

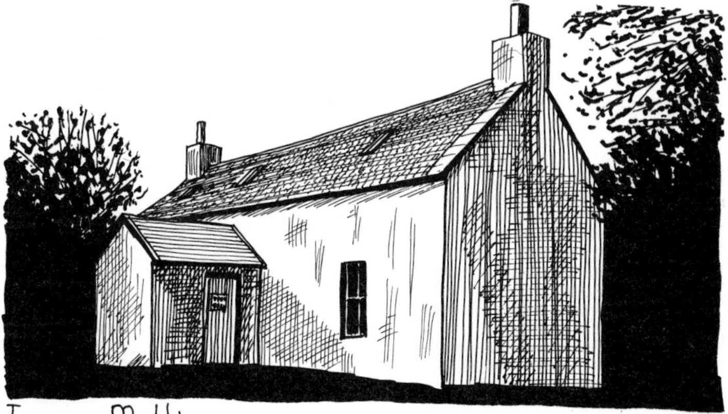

Inver Mallie

Loch Arkaig

Continued →

50

200 m

150 m

substantial
plank bridge
ford
Inver Mallie
fords
ford
gate
100 m
fishing hut
pl. bridge
50 m
suspension
bridge
200 m
dead
pines
(→ -sad!)

N

1 km

Continued ↑

opposite ↑

Continued ↓

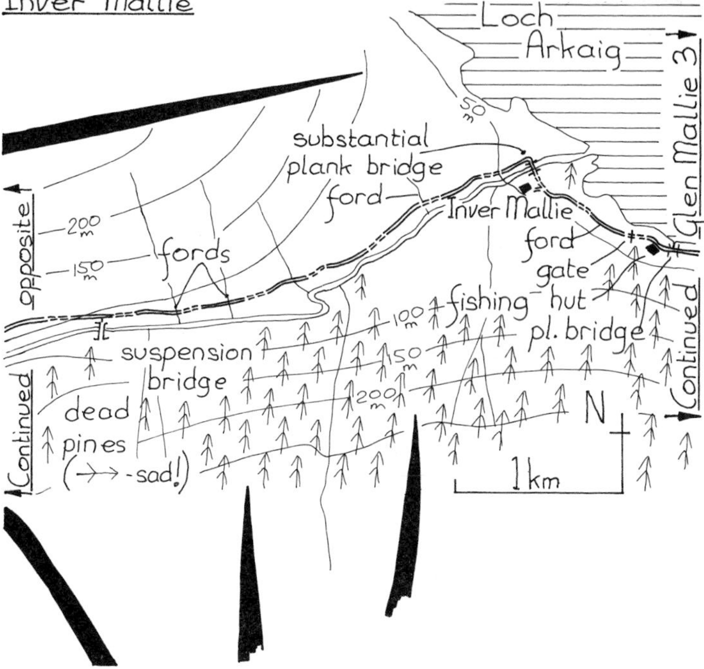

Glen Mallie 3

Loch Arkaig.

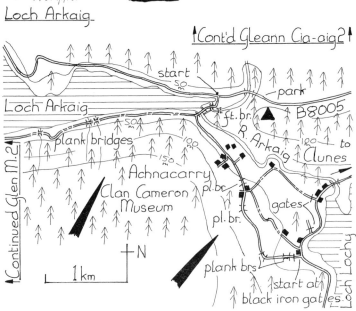

The Glen Dessarry tracks, together with Glen Pean form the westward extensions to the tortuous Loch Arkaig road. The tree-planting spoils the desolate nature of the glen, yet provides tracks giving cycle access to the upper glen, about 6km or 4miles above Strathan. A path continues via Sourlies bothy and the ruined settlement at Carnoch, over Mam Meadail and on to Inverie..... no-go for bikes! Glen Dessarry also has links with Glen Kingie and Glen Finnan for those on foot only, and Glen Pean, a small part of which can be cycled. There is shelter at A'Chuil bothy, some 200m below the track, and at Sourlies bothy. Camping is permitted at Sourlies but discouraged elsewhere.

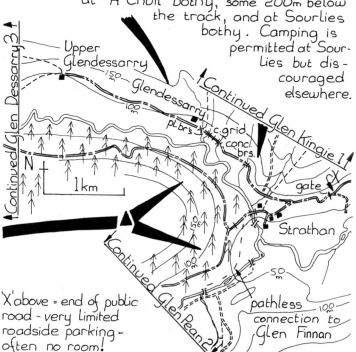

'X' above = end of public road - very limited roadside parking - often no room!

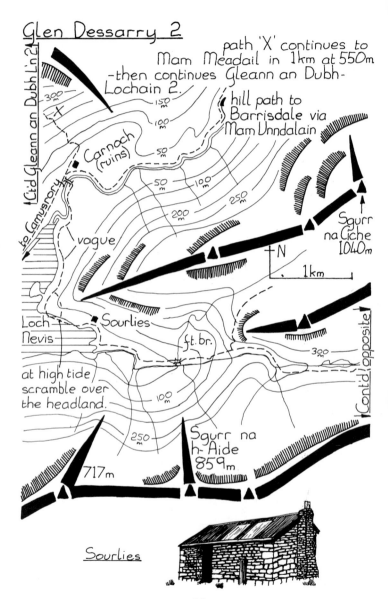

Glen Dessarry 2

path 'X' continues to Mam Meadail in 1km at 550m —then continues Gleann an Dubh-Lochain 2.

'Ctd Gleann an Dubh Ln 2'

300

150

100

hill path to Barrisdale via Mam Unndalain

Carnoch (ruins)

50

50 100

250

200
m

to Camusrory

vague

N

1 km

Sgurr na Ciche 1040m

Loch Nevis

Sourlies

ft. br.

300
m

at high tide scramble over the headland.

100
m

250
m

Sgurr na h-Aide 859m

717m

'Contd opposite'

Sourlies

Beyond the trees and north of the glen are some
serious mountains, culminating in Sgurr na Ciche,
all of which have been explored by your author
en route from Glen Finnan to Inverie (but not all
in a day!). However, the low level walk over
Bealach an Lagain Duibh ('Y' below) is superb
in its own right. This is rough, wild country
indeed – to be enjoyed whilst leaving no trace
of one's passing, but never rushed, only to be
ticked off in a book as 'done'; such country deserves
better!

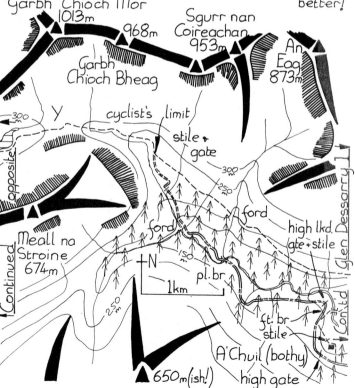

67

Glen Pean 1

The route up Glen Pean starts from Strathan at the head of Loch Arkaig - see Glen Dessarry 1 on page 63. Only a small portion of the route is possible with a bike; the remainder provides one of the most exciting low level walks your author and his 'better half' have ever done. Care is needed on the path above the south side of Lochan Leum an t- Sagairt -'X' below-as it

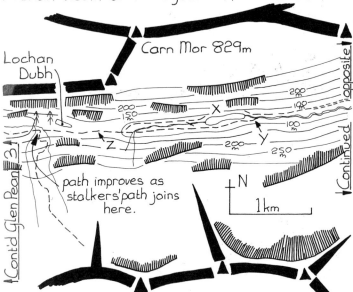

crosses steep slopes. Just before the lochan - at Y-go up the steep bank on the left (heading West). A similar manoeuvre, at Z, avoids the spooky silted Lochan Dubh. A path does run around the north side of Lochan L. an t-S. but this is even more precarious. If you lose the path, hunt around for it, off the path the going is very rough. Strathan to Oban bothy is 14 km or 9 miles.

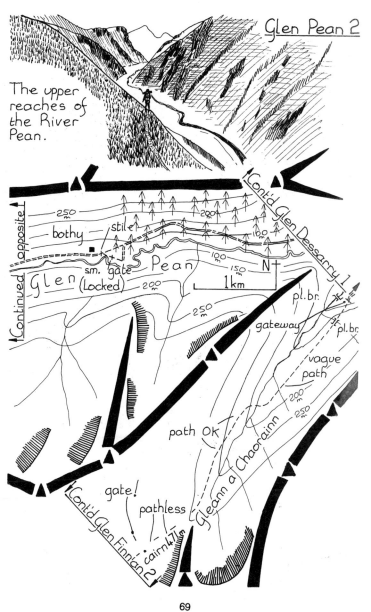

The upper reaches of the River Pean.

250 m

bothy

stile

200 m

Glen

sm. gate (Locked)

Pean

100 m

150 m

200 m

250 m

N

1km

160 m

pl.br.

gateway

pl.br.

vague path

200 m

250 m

path OK

Gleann a Chaorainn

gate!

pathless

cairn 471 m

Continued opposite

Cont'd Glen Dessarry 1

Cont'd Glen Finnan 2

Glen Pean 3

Oban

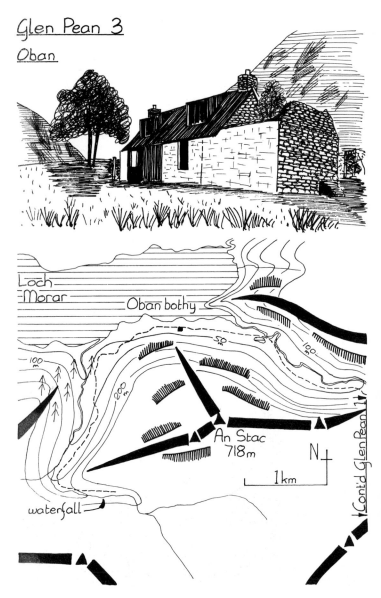

Loch Morar

Oban bothy

100 m

100 m

50 m

200 m

An Stac
718 m

waterfall

N

1 km

Cont'd Glen Pean

Gleann Suileag lies to the north of Loch Eil and is accessible from either Fassfern or the forest track a mile or so to the east. The current O.S. map also shows a connection to Loch Eil station but your author found no such link to the east loop track. These forest tracks, elevated high above Loch Eil, give superb views of The Ben above Fort Bill. The tracks can be cycled almost to Glensulaig bothy from which point a rough and in places indistinct path crosses the watershed to Glen Loy. This centre section makes the through trip impractical with a bike. The tracks to the west of Fassfern are short, steep, and run only to dead-ends. The direct route, one way, from Fassfern to the end of the track is 5 km or 3 miles. Return by the eastern loop including the last mile or so on the road is 13km or 8 miles. Direct distance from Fassfern to the road in Glen Loy is 12km or 7.5miles; a pleasant plod if transport can be arranged. The bothy is usually open so shelter is available.

Gleann Suileag 2

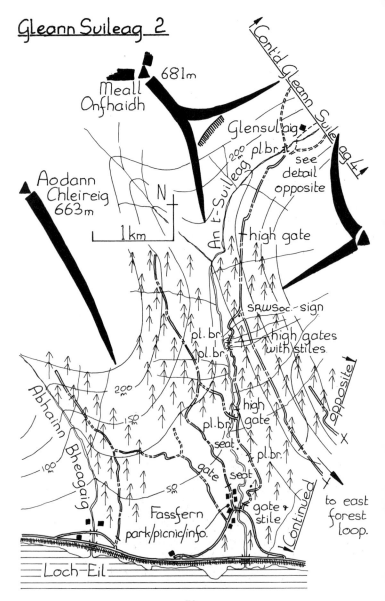

Meall Onfhaidh 681m

Glensulaig

200m pl.br.

see detail opposite

Aodann Chleireig 663m

N

1km

high gate

An t-Suileag

SRWSoc. sign

pl. br.

high gates with stiles

pl. br.

200m

150

100

high gate

pl. br.

seat

Abhainn Bheagaig

gate

opposite

X

50m

seat

pl. br.

gate + stile

Fassfern park/picnic/info.

Continued

to east forest loop.

Loch Eil

Cont'd Gleann Suileag 4

The environs of Glensulaig

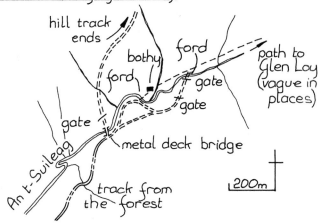

hill track ends

bothy

ford

ford

ford

path to Glen Loy (vague in places)

gate

gate

gate

An t-Suileag

metal deck bridge

track from the forest

200m

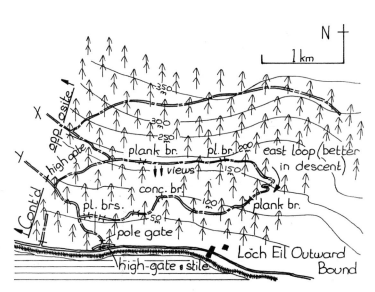

N

1 km

350

300

250

camp site

high gate

plank br.

pl. br.

200

east loop (better in descent)

views

150

conc. br.

pl. brs.

100

plank br.

Cont'd

50

pole gate

high-gate • stile

Loch Eil Outward Bound

X

Y

73

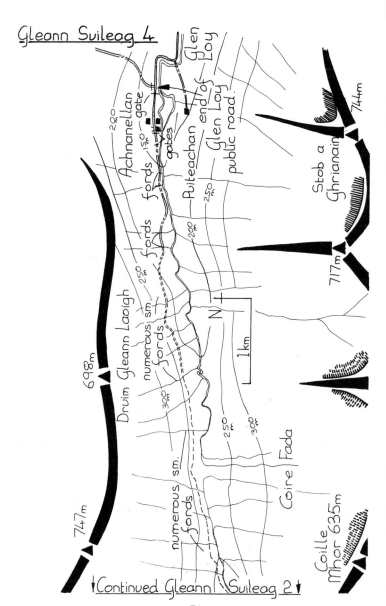

Glen Loy

Achnanellan
gate
fords
gates
Puiteachan
end of
Glen Loy
public road.

200
150m
250m

Druim Gleann Laoigh
fords
numerous sm. fords
300m
200m
250m

N+

1km

numerous sm. fords
250m
300m
250m

Coire Fada

744m
Stob a Ghrianain
717m

698m
747m

Coille Mhor 635m

↓ Continued Gleann Suileag 2 ↓

Gleann Fionnlighe provides a somewhat brief excursion on an old right of way which soon becomes pathless. [The route then crosses Gleann Camgharaidh and descends into Gleann a Chaorainn bound for Glen Pean and Strathan - alas all pathless and inferior to the Glen Finnan approach to Strathan.] The rough track is rideable as far as the last bridge, 6·5 km (4 miles) from the start. There is shelter in an old shed just past Wauchan and unless you are seeking out the old right of way, return is by the same route.

no connection to Gleann Dubh Lighe 314m

ends

shed

Cont'd G. Fionnlighe 2

100

high gate · stile

plank bridge

Wauchan

plank bridges

Beinn an t-Sneachda 625m

N

1 km

100 150

locked pole gate

stone bridge

(old road)

head of Loch Eil

50 m

A830

parking spot

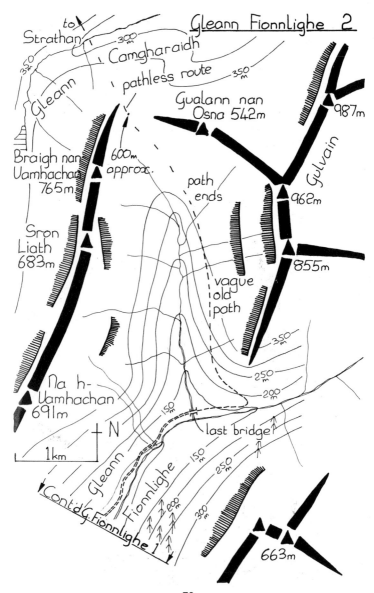

to
Strathan
Camgharaidh
300 m
350
Gleann
pathless route
350 m
Gualann nan
Osna 542m
987m
Braigh nan
Uamhachan
765m
600m
approx.
path
ends
Gulvain
962m
Sron
Liath
683m
vague
old
path
855m
350
250
Na h-
Uamhachan
691m
200 m
N
150
1km
last bridge
Gleann
150
250
Cont'd G. Fionnlighe 1
Fionnlighe
200 m
300 m
663m

Gleann Dubh Lighe

Gleann Dubh Lighe is sandwiched between Gleann Fionnlighe and Glen Finnan and its pathless upper reaches run into Gleann Camgharaidh over the watershed at Lochan Chomhlain. The short walk or cycle, via the bothy, gives access to Streap, a fine mountain dominating the head of the glen and also towering over the Glen Finnan watershed. Those with an energy surplus can try the track 'X' which rises at a ludicrous gradient only to run to a disappointing dead end; surveyed of course by yours truly -all in the interest of accuracy -it is steep enough to hurt!

844m

Beinn an Tuim 810m

high gate

X

bothy

pl.br.

highgt.

314m

Gleann

Dubh Lighe

200 m

150 m

150 m

Drimsallie Mill

1 km

high gate

gate

50 m

100 m

park

A830

N

Glen Finnan 1

The 'track' up Glen Finnan is, almost as far as the
bothy, a metalled road. The lower glen is dominated
by the viaduct and the upper glen is overlooked by the
strangely suburban-looking house - but what a posit-
ion! Shelter is available at the bothy - even light!
A track continues giving excellent cycle access
for hillwalkers
though the
going gets
tough a
mile

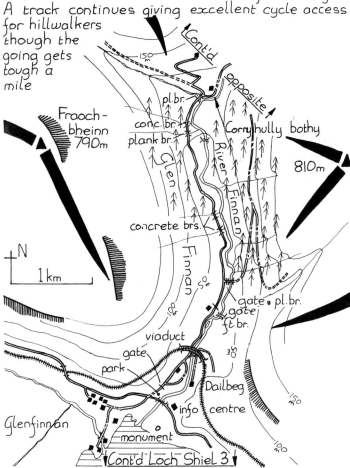

Cont'd

opposite

150 m

pl.br.

Fraoch-
bheinn
790m

conc.br.

plank br.

Corryhully bothy

Glen

River Finnan

810m

concrete brs.

N

1 km

Finnan

50

100

gate. pl.br.

gate
ft.br.

viaduct

gate

park

30

Dailbeg

info centre

150

Glenfinnan

monument

100

info

Cont'd Loch Shiel 3

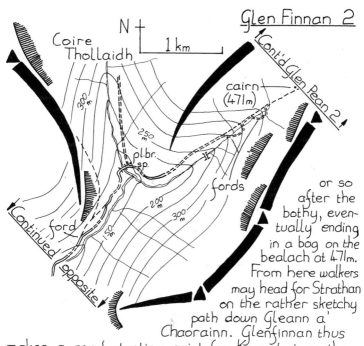

N

1 km

Coire Tholllaidh

cairn (471m)

Cont'd Glen Pean 2

pl.br.
sp.

fords

Continued ford

Continued opposite

or so after the bothy, eventually ending in a bog on the bealach at 471m. From here walkers may head for Strathan on the rather sketchy path down Gleann a' Chaorainn. Glenfinnan thus makes a good starting point for Knoydart as the boat from Inverie to Mallaig, and the train, can be used for the return to Glenfinnan or Fort Bill".

Corryhully

Borrodale Burn 1

The Arisaig-Kinloid-Scamadale-Borrodale Burn
track and path may be enjoyed in two ways:-
Arisaig to Scamadale is easily ridden
at midge-beating speed as a
short bike ride of only
14km or 8miles return.
The full loop via
the Burn takes
in a gem of a
path requiring
careful navig-
ation and an
O.S. map. The
reward is an
ever-changing
scene
with

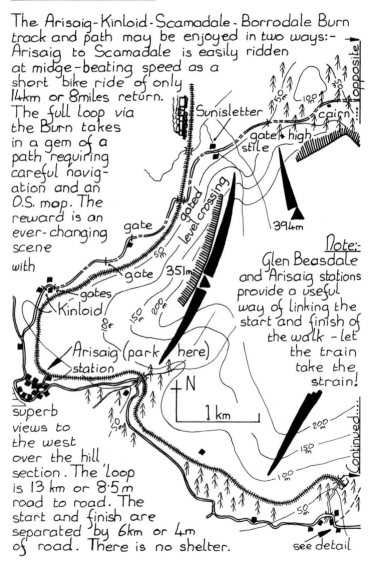

Sunisletter

gate high
stile

cairn

394m

351m

level crossing

gated

gate

gate

gates
Kinloid

Arisaig (park here)
station

N

1 km

Note:-
Glen Beasdale
and Arisaig stations
provide a useful
way of linking the
start and finish of
the walk - let
the train
take the
strain!

200m
150m
100m
50m

superb
views to
the west
over the hill
section. The loop
is 13 km or 8·5 m
road to road. The
start and finish are
separated by 6km or 4m
of road. There is no shelter.

see detail

opposite

Continued

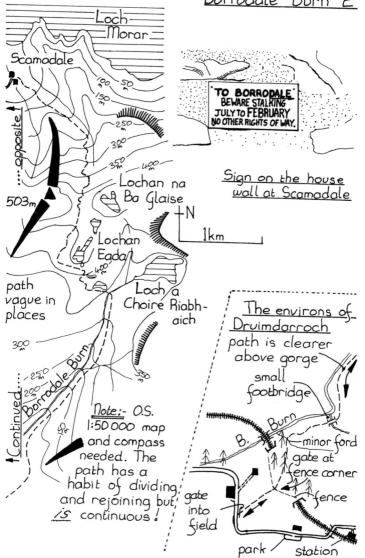

Loch Morar

Scamadale

opposite

100m
50m
150m
250m
300m
350m
400m

503m

Lochan na Ba Glaise

N

1km

Lochan Eada

400m

path vague in places

Loch a Choire Riabhaich

300m

250m
200m

Borrodale Burn

350m

Continued...

Note:- O.S. 1:50 000 map and compass needed. The path has a habit of dividing and rejoining but *is* continuous!

'TO BORRODALE' BEWARE STALKING JULY TO FEBRUARY NO OTHER RIGHTS OF WAY.

Sign on the house wall at Scamadale

The environs of Druimdarroch
path is clearer above gorge
small footbridge
B. Burn
minor ford
gate at fence corner
fence
gate into field
park
station

81

Glen Tarbet 1

Glen Tarbet is only 1km long, between Tarbet Bay and South Tarbet Bay. It is reached by a foot-path along the north shore of Loch Morar. The route is an easy walk and can be covered one way using the Mallaig-Inverie ferry service which also calls at Tarbet. Indeed, your author did this walk some 15 years ago with his wife and (then) young son and daughter. Little did we realise that we would return to survey the path for a guide book - never mind the eighth in a series. How life can change - and improve - my writing really is a labour of love.... Stop this waffle man and get on with it!! The one-way distance from the end of the public road to Tarbet pier is 9km or 6 miles. There is shelter from the west coast rain at Tarbet.

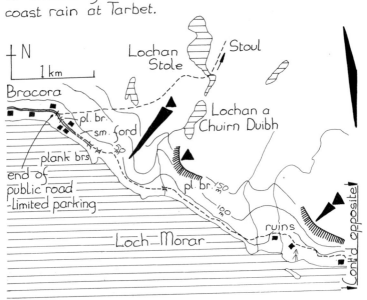

N

1 km

Bracora

Lochan Stole

Stoul

Lochan a Chuirn Duibh

pl. br.

sm. ford

plank brs

end of public road -limited parking

pl. br.

ruins

Loch Morar

Cont'd opposite

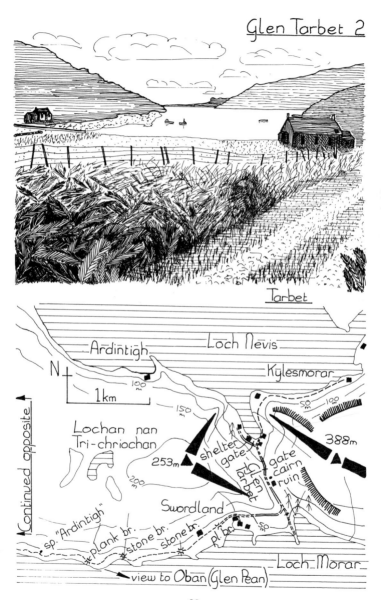

Tarbet

Loch Nevis

Ardintigh

Kylesmorar

N

1km

100

150

Lochan nan
Tri-chriochan

50 100

shelter
gate

388m

253m

200
300

Glen Tarbet

gate
cairn
ruin

Swordland

sp. "Ardintigh"   plank br.   stone br.   stone br.   pl. br.   50

Loch Morar

view to Oban (Glen Pean)

Continued opposite ►

Ardnamurchan to Ardgour

Rubha Aird	91
Loch Shiel	94
Glen Hurich	97
Glen Scaddle	100
Cona Glen	104

Ardnamurchan to Ardgour

Access:- This area lies south of the Fort William to Mallaig road, west of Loch Linnhe and north of Glen Tarbert, Strontian and Loch Sunart. Access is inconvenient - which together with a complete absence of Munros keeps the area peaceful and quiet. There are five points of access:- Lochailort is the start of the south-bound coast road; Glenfinnan provides bike access (via Loch Shiel); the south Loch Eil road also leaves the A830 near Glenfinnan ; the Corran Ferry provides the shortest access ; Strontian is accessible from Lochaline via Mull by ferry.

Accommodation:- A thin sprinkling of B,B's etc. lies around the perimeter of the area, the main centre being the **exceedingly** pleasant village of Strontian which has just the right amount of everything and avoids any hint of 'tackiness'. Lochailort, Glenuig, Acharacle and Corran all have more B.B's as does the beautiful Ardnamurchan peninsula.

Geographical Features:- The area can be divided into two : the Ardnamurchan peninsula in the west and the mountainous area forming the major part of the region to the east. The glens are long, steep sided and, around Loch Shiel, clothed in forest. These long glens link together to provide opportunities for long sorties into the wilds - tempered by some (seemingly needless?) restrictions for cycles.

Mountains:- The area is without Munros, however the fact that none of the mountains reach the magical 3000ft contour adds to, rather than detracts from its appeal; there are very few paths high on the mountains. Those hills flanking Loch Shiel are exceptionally wild, rugged and remote requiring either wild camps or extremely long days out to even begin their thorough exploration. Not only are many glens pathless, they are defended by some of the worst tussocks your author has ever encountered; huge wobbling mounds each with its own moat!!

Rivers:- The longest river in the region is the Cona which is joined by the Scaddle just before it drains into Loch Linnhe. The Moidart, Gour and Hurich are of comparable size, not all the respective glens are easy to explore and the more than ample rainfall ensures river crossings are always a major consideration on cross-country treks.

Forests:- The forests of Loch Shiel and Glen Hurich provide the best mountainbiking in the area - indeed the Loch Shiel track is a viable alternative to the coast road apart from the enormous hill between Polloch and Strontian.

Lochs:- Loch Sunart cuts deep into the area - all the way to Strontian. Only Glen Tarbert separates this from Loch Linnhe, which is of course the southern continuation of the Great Glen fault. Loch Linnhe continues, as a sea loch into Loch Eil and these two lochs conspire to make access to the region as difficult as possible! Loch Shiel is a superb natural (no dams here!) fresh water loch lying diagonally across the region thankfully devoid of road noise yet all enjoyable by bike - the track giving fine views across to the loch's wild north west shoreline.

Emergency:- Apart from the tame Rubha Aird route all glens lead well away from public roads and need treating with respect. Even a broken bike half way along Loch Shiel can be serious. Also - mind those river crossings!

Ardnamurchan to Ardgour Routes 1

Rubha Aird

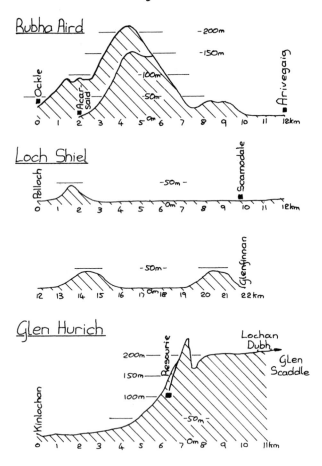

Loch Shiel

Glen Hurich

Ardnamurchan to Ardgour Routes 2

Glen Scaddle

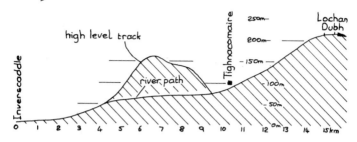

Cona Glen

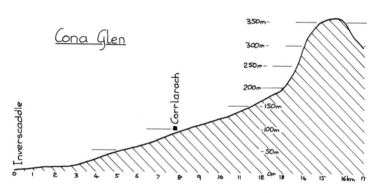

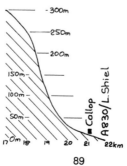

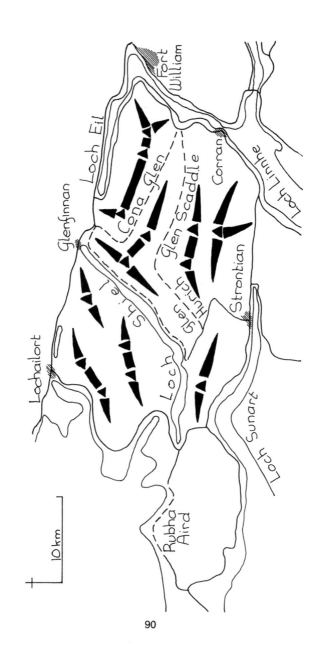

Fort William
Loch Eil
Loch Linnhe
Corran
Cona Glen
Glen Scaddle
Glenfinnan
Glen Hurich
Strontian
Loch Shiel
Lochailort
Loch Sunart
Rubha Aird
10 km

This route explores the wild north coast of the Ardnamurchan peninsula, between Ockle in the west and Arivegaig to the east. It can be tackled as an out-and-back walk from either end; a through walk of 12km or 7.5 miles end to end if transport can be arranged; or a mountainbike circuit of some 53km (33miles) which includes some pleasant road cycling via Glenborrodale. The path section of just under 3km or 2miles will have to be walked to prevent erosion. This path section is easier (or less difficult!) if covered east to west - making an anti-clockwise circuit. There are tea stops at Glenbeg and Glenborrodale but no shelter on the off-road section. Forest, beaches, hill path, and if the 'circuit' is ridden, quiet roads - all in a day..... superb!

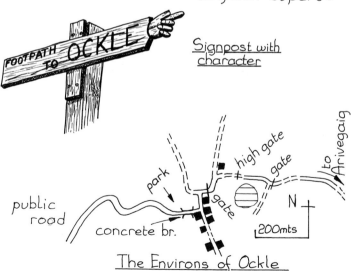

<u>Signpost with character</u>

<u>The Environs of Ockle</u>

public road

park

concrete br.

high gate

gate

gate

to Arivegaig

N

200mts

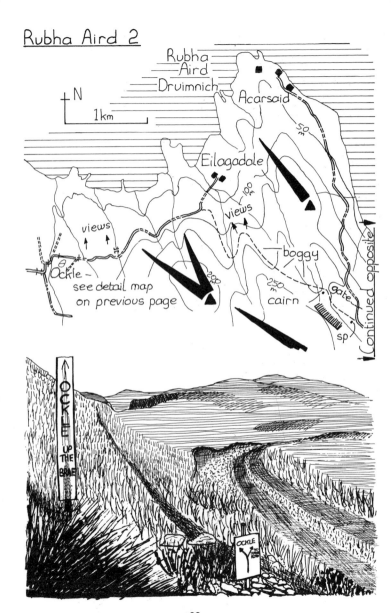

Rubha Aird 2

Rubha
Aird
Druimnich

Acarsaid

Eilagadale

50 m

100 m

views

views

boggy

250 m

200 m

cairn

Ockle –
see detail map
on previous page

gate

sp

continued opposite

N
1km

OCKLE
UP THE
BRAE

OCKLE
UP THE
BRAE

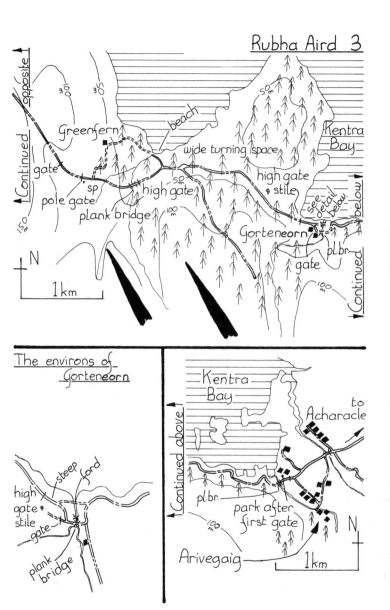

Loch Shiel 1

The track alongside Loch Shiel extends for some 22 km or 14 miles from Polloch in the south to Glen Finnan in the north. The loch is connected to Glen Hurich by a short length of public road alongside the picturesque but unfortunately named Loch Doilet. At the northern end the Callop path links Loch Shiel with Cona Glen. These connections are a no-go for bikes as a) they are very rough and b) bikes are banned in Cona Glen and Glen Scaddle. However, Cona Glen, Callop, Loch Shiel, Loch Doilet, Glen Hurich and Glen Scaddle makes a low level walk of some 73km or 46 miles including a night or two en-route. See Link Route 4 for more details.

← Continued → opposite

Gorstanvorran

150

Loch Shiel

Maman Odhar

100 m

N

1km

150 m

100 m

path to viewpoint - well worth a look!

50 m

C.grid gte

parking

to a dead end

Polloch (uninspiring)

150 m

100 m

Torran nam Mial

to Strontian (via 1000 ft. hill!)

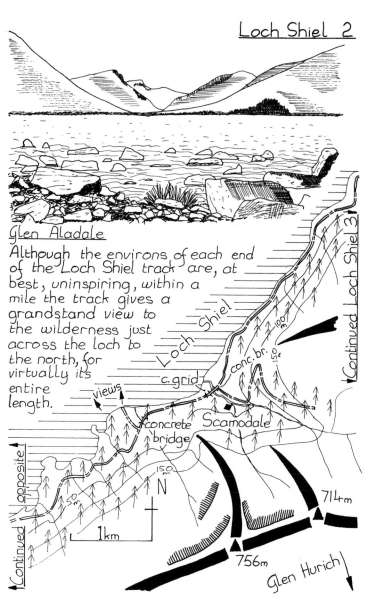

Glen Aladale

Although the environs of each end of the Loch Shiel track are, at best, uninspiring, within a mile the track gives a grandstand view to the wilderness just across the loch to the north, for virtually its entire length.

Loch Shiel

Continued Loch Shiel 3

conc. br.
c. grid
views
concrete bridge
Scamodale
Continued opposite

N

1km

150m
50m

714m
756m

Glen Hurich

Loch Shiel 3

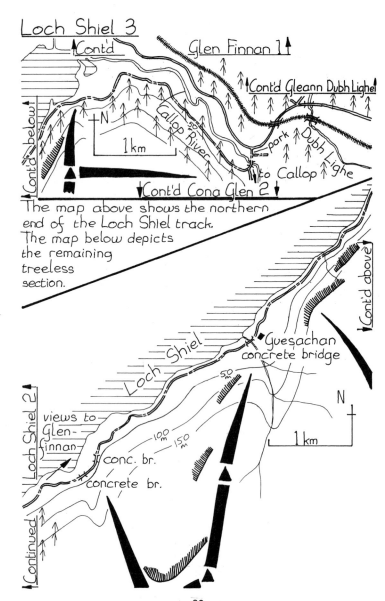

Glen Finnan 1↑

↑Cont'd Gleann Dubh Lighe

↑Cont'd below

Callop River

↑park

Dubh Lighe

to Callop

N

1 km

↓Cont'd Cona Glen 2↓

The map above shows the northern
end of the Loch Shiel track.
The map below depicts
the remaining
treeless
section.

Cont'd above→

Loch Shiel

Guesachan
concrete bridge

Loch Shiel 2

views to
Glen-
finnan

conc. br.

concrete br.

Continued

N

1 km

96

Glen Hurich lies east and a little north of Loch Doilet, access being over the hill from Strontian. Careful study of the following map pages should precede any trip into the glen, to decide which side of the glen to explore. A new track now extends well into the upper glen on the south side. If a through walk to Glen Scaddle is planned either:- ① use this south side track to its limit and either cross the river at the outflow of Lochan Dubh, or walk around the pathless south side of Lochan Dubh to gain the path or:- ② battle your way out of the woods above Resourie and follow the path on the north side all the way, noting the vague section of path with care. Bikes are not allowed in Glen Scaddle and in any event the watershed is too rough to qualify as a bike ride. The bothy is buried deep in the woods and some 250m from the track - and about 6km or 4miles from the public road. Refer to Link Route 4 for details of an extended walk.

The environs of Resourie

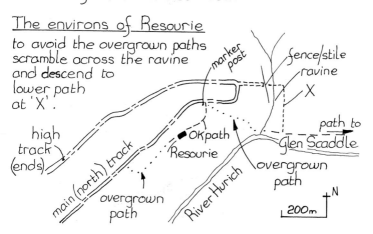

to avoid the overgrown paths scramble across the ravine and descend to lower path at 'X'.

marker post

fence/stile

ravine

X

path to Glen Scaddle

high track (ends)

main (north) track

OKpath

Resourie

overgrown path

River Hurich

overgrown path

overgrown path

N

200m

Glen Hurich 2

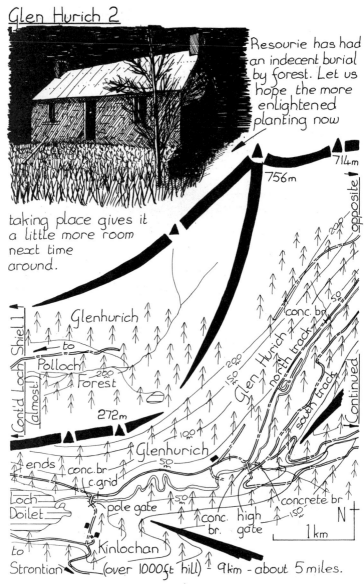

Resourie has had an indecent burial by forest. Let us hope the more enlightened planting now taking place gives it a little more room next time around.

714m

756m

opposite

Glenhurich

conc. br

Glen Hurich

north track

Cont'd Loch Shiel 1

to Polloch Forest (almost!)

200

Continued

200

150

south track

272m

100

50

Glenhurich

50

ends

conc. br

l. c. grid

50

concrete br

150

Loch Doilet

pole gate

50

conc. high br. gate

N

1 km

to Strontian

Kinlochan (over 1000ft hill) 9km - about 5 miles.

98

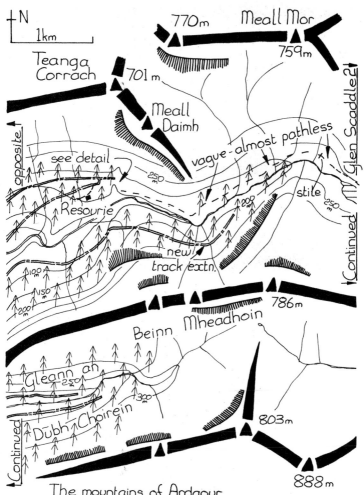

The mountains of Ardgour
fail to reach the magic 3000ft (914m) contour, but
are rugged and remote. What matter that they
are a few feet short? Enjoy them as they are!

Glen Scaddle 1

Cycles are not allowed in Glen Scaddle, or indeed neighbouring Cona Glen. However, all is not lost as there are more possibilities for walkers. The long through hike to Glen Hurich (25 km or 16 miles road to road) is a committing walk though shelter is at hand at a shed 1km above Tighnacomaire and, in Glen Hurich, Resourie. Take care planning your route into Glen Hurich. The paths shown in Glen Scaddle on the current O.S. 1:50000 map are misleading. A major ford and rough pathless river bank are avoided by taking the track through the woods which rises above the mid section of the south side of the glen. Experienced walkers can return via Cona Glen by climbing very steeply to the gate on the col at X and using the river crossing Y in Cona Glen; a circuit of 34km or 21miles but not recommended if rivers are high as one could end up trapped at the wrong side of Cona River. Enjoy your walk - I hope it stays fine!

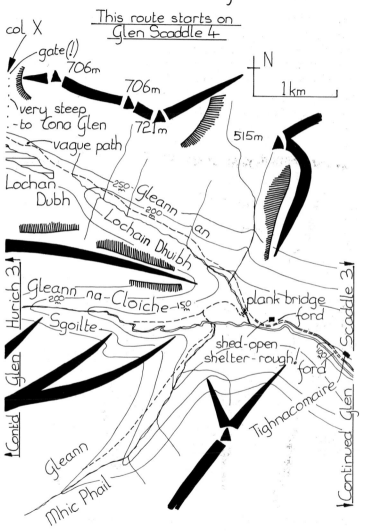

This route starts on
Glen Scaddle 4

col X

gate(!)

706m

706m

721m

515m

N

1 km

very steep
-to Cona Glen

vague path

Lochan
Dubh

250 m

Gleann

an

200 m

Lochain Dhuibh

Gleann na-Cloiche

200 m

150 m

plank bridge

ford

Sgoilte

shed-open
shelter-rough!

ford

Tighnacomaire

100 m

Gleann

Mhic Phail

‹ Cont'd Glen Hurich 3 ›

‹ Continued Glen Scaddle 3 ›

Glen Scaddle 3

Your author and his 'better half' surveyed Cona Glen and Glen Scaddle all in a day including the watershed leading north from Cona Glen to Callop, the "gated col" (X) and the head of Gleann Lochain Duibh; a long day of almost 25 miles of walking plus all the note-taking and record photography. What better occupation could we pursue?..... Refer to Link Route 4 for details of even longer sorties into this wild region.

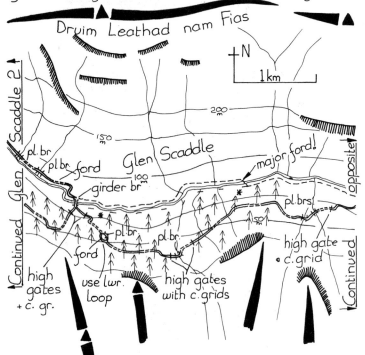

"O.S." path" *-* is rough/vague/missing - I didn't find it!!

It is essential that gates on the upper track are SHUT

The signpost below requests that walkers keep to
the riverbank. Your author arrived at this point
from the high woodland track guilt free after
shutting the gates behind him. Whilst failing to
appreciate the damage a sensible walker can
inflict upon the woodland track your author is
obliged to ask his readers to
comply with the request and
do battle with the rough
riverbank path beyond
(west of) the ford.
Cyclists are
banned.
Why?

Continued Cona Glen 4

Cona River

River Scaddle

opposite

150m
100m
50m

Creagbheitheachain
(ruin)

150m
100m
50m

gate • stile

pl. brs.

N

100m

1km

signpost

150m

Continued

pl. br.

to
Corran
6km/4m

596m

598m

Cona Glen 1

I do wish landowners would explain, on their many signposts *why* they ban cycles*. Cona Glen would have been ideal for a bike ride were it not for the restrictions. Ah well! Walkers, however have the options of extending the trip via Callop to Glenfinnan and beyond - see Link Route 2.4. Cona Glen even provides the walker with a long approach to Knoydart from the Corran ferry via Glenfinnan and Strathan. An interesting, mostly pathless right of way runs from the head of Cona Glen via Bealach Sgriodain, just west of O.S. spot height 701m to descend steeply to Resourie in Glen Hurich. A further 'escape' route from the head of Cona Glen is via the col at X to Glen Scaddle (refer to Glen S.2). This involves a river crossing (Y) which may be difficult or impossible, a slog up to the col, and a very steep descent (on grass) to the outlet of Lochan Dubh. Only experienced hillwalkers should make the crossing to Scaddle. There is shelter at the head of the glen, and a shed at Corrlarach. One-way distance from the road to the river crossing Y is 14 km or 9 miles. Distance from the same road (at Inver Scaddle) to the main road at Glenfinnan is 21 km or 13.5 miles. There is excellent hillwalking on very rough peaks all around the glen head — solitude almost guaranteed due to the remote location and the absence of 3000ft peaks - not a Munro-bagger in sight!

* How about:- "No cycles because ...."
    or:- "No cycles beyond......."
  or even :- "Cyclists keep to the track"
or(honestly):- "No cyclists because the landowner just doesn't like them" !!

Cona Glen 2

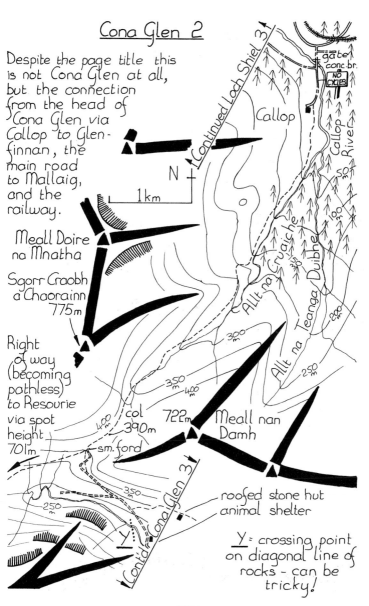

Despite the page title this is not Cona Glen at all, but the connection from the head of Cona Glen via Callop to Glenfinnan, the main road to Mallaig, and the railway.

N

1 km

Continued Loch Shiel 3

Callop

gate
conc. br.
NO CYCLES

Callop River

30

Allt na Cruaiche

Allt na Teanga Duibhe

100

150

200

250

300 m

Meall Doire na Mnatha

Sgorr Craobh a Chaorainn 775m

Right of way (becoming pathless) to Resourie via spot height 701m

350 m

400

300 m

400

col 390m

sm. ford

722m

Meall nan Damh

250 m

350

250

Continued Cona Glen 3

roofed stone hut animal shelter

Y = crossing point on diagonal line of rocks - can be tricky!

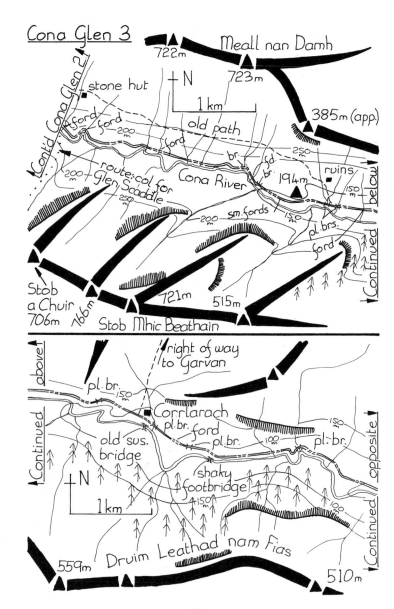

Cona Glen 3

Meall nan Damh
722m
723m
Cont'd Cona Glen 2
stone hut
385m (app.)
N
1 km
ford
ford
old path
200
ford
200
br.
250
route: col for
Glen Scaddle
Cona River
194m
ruins
200
250
150
200
sm. fords
150
Continued below
200
pl. brs.
ford
Stob
a Chuir
706m
766m
721m
515m
Stob Mhic Beathain

Continued above
right of way
to Garvan
pl. br.
150
Corrlarach
pl. br. ford
pl. br.
150
Continued
100
pl. br.
old sus.
bridge
100
N
shaky
footbridge
1 km
150
100
Continued opposite
Druim Leathad nam Fias
559m
510m

106

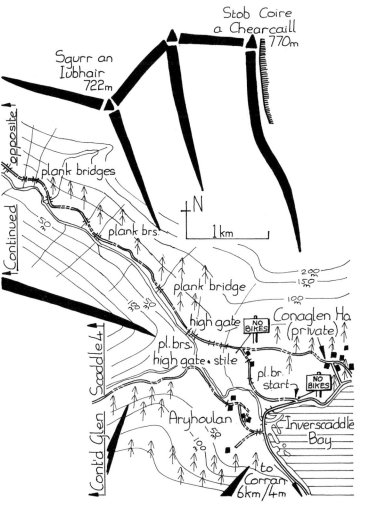

Stob Coire
a Chearcaill
770m

Sgurr an
Iubhair
722m

opposite

Continued

plank bridges

plank brs.

50
30

N

1 km

plank bridge

200
150
100

100

high gate

NO BIKES

Conaglen Ho.
(private)

100
50
30

pl. brs.
high gate · stile

pl. br.
start

NO BIKES

Scaddle 4

Cont'd Glen Scaddle 4

Aryhoulan

100
50

Inverscaddle
Bay

to
Corran
6km/4m

107

Morvern

Glen Cripesdale 115
Auliston Point 119
Gleann Dubh 122
Loch Teacuis 126
Savary Glen 128

Morvern

Access:- Morvern is even more inaccessible than the preceding section - hence its charm. Lying between the Sound of Mull and Loch Linnhe, Morvern is almost severed from the mainland by Loch Sunart. The peninsula is strangely attached to the rest of mainland Scotland by a glen - Glen Tarbert - rather than by higher ground. Access is via either Corran Ferry or the Lochaline ferry from Mull if the long drive around Loch Eil or via Lochailort is to be avoided.

Accommodation:- Within Morvern not much accommodation is available apart from Lochaline and a few B.B's dotted along the Drimnin road. There is an excellent campsite almost on the beach at Fiunary (offering the best chance of a midge free camp from June to August!). Strontian, just outwith the region has everything, including an info. centre.

Geographical Features:- Morvern is a wild, mountainous peninsula, little of which can be appreciated from the public roads. Large areas of moor and mountain make up its interior, some of which is clothed with forest. With its ferry connections Morvern, like Knapdale and Kintyre in Book 5, feels very much like an island.

Mountains:- No Munros, but to the east lie some fine hills. Creach Bheinn being the highest closely followed by Fuar Bheinn and Beinn Mheadhoin. West of the Gleann Geal road, the hills don't even reach 2000ft, but the tracks reach almost as high as anyone cycling the Savary Glen circuit will testify! The escarpment above Loch Arienas is noteworthy

Rivers:- The region is bordered by the River Tarbert, to the north, and the central region is drained by the Black Water in Gleann Dubh and the Abhainn a Ghlinne Ghil in Gleann Geal. These join forces and, oddly at the outlet of Loch Arienas, become the River Aline, amid a confusion of old and new bridges. Other burns in the region are short; there are no serious river crossings to be negotiated in Morvern.

Forests :- The two main areas of forest are at Savary Glen, continuing around the Aoineadh Mor/Beag escarpment to the Barr River, and around Glen Cripesdale, together providing the region's best mountainbiking on the forest tracks. Apart from odd lumps of plantation in Gleann Geal, which have no worthwhile tracks there are no other significant areas of forest. The south shore of Loch Sunart, being sheltered from the prevailing south-westerly gales, has natural birchwoods - a rare feature on the mostly exposed west coast.

Lochs :- Loch Arienas is the largest fresh water loch, fed by Loch Doire nam Mart. This loch drains into the River Aline. Sea lochs Loch Sunart, Loch Teacuis, Loch Aline and Loch a Choire in the east all indent the coastline, but without the fjord-like drama of the northern lochs in this book.

Emergency :- All tracks provide a quick exit to the public road and civilisation. Glen Cripesdale and its hill path are quite remote. Sensible precautions and conduct will ensure safe enjoyment of the region.

Morvern Routes 1

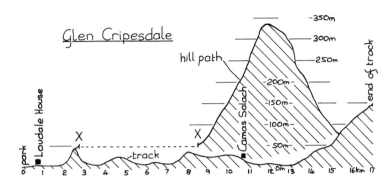

Glen Cripesdale

hill path

Laudale House
park
track
Camas Salach
end of track

-350m
300m
250m
-200m-
-150m-
-100m-
-50m-
0m

0 park
1 2 3 4 5 6 7 8 9 10 11 12 13 14 15 16km 17

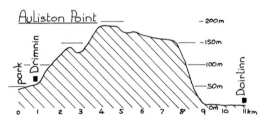

Auliston Point

park
Drimnin
Doirlinn

-200m
-150m
100m
50m
0m

0 1 2 3 4 5 6 7 8 9 10 11km

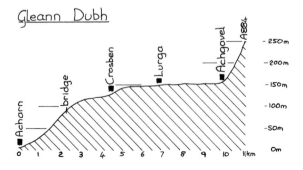

Gleann Dubh

Acharn
bridge
Crosben
Lurga
Achagavel
A884

-250m
-200m
-150m
-100m
-50m
0m

0 1 2 3 4 5 6 7 8 9 10 11km

Loch Teacuis

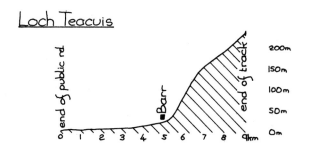

Savary Glen

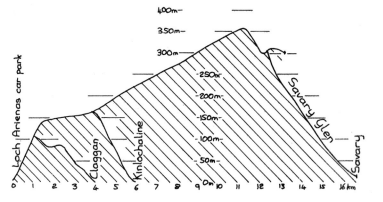

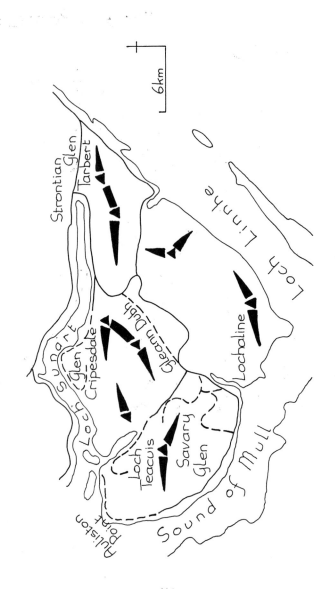

Glen Cripesdale 1

The start of the coastal route into Glen Cripesdale lies some 10km or 6miles (by road) south of Strontian and explores much of the southern shore of the beautiful Loch Sunart, before turning east into the Glen. The public road ends 1km east of Laudale House but the route can easily be cycled in a day from the A884 junction at Liddesdale or even from Strontian. New forest roads have complicated the area around Glencripesdale as detailed below. One suspects more forest tracks may appear! A hill path is available to walkers who may wish to vary the return leg - the hill section is not a bike ride. There is no shelter. Distances are as set out below:-

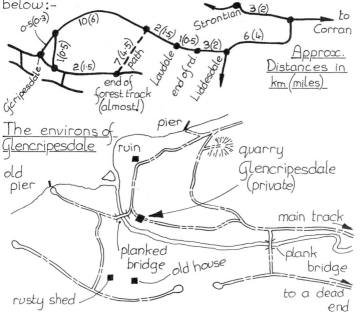

Approx. Distances in km (miles)

The environs of Glencripesdale

Glen Cripesdale 2

Note how Glen Cripesdale (the glen) is two words, but this becomes Glencripesdale (the 'big house') and Glencripesdale Burn – a common phenomenon in Scottish place names. Note also the path X, below, to Loch Teacuis, via Bealach Sloc an Eich – obliterated by clear felling the trees.

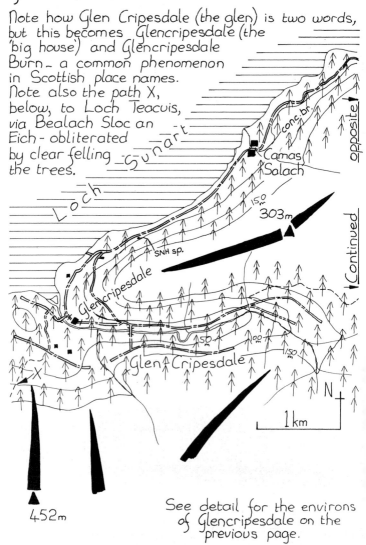

opposite ►

Continued ►

Loch Sunart

conc. br.

Camas Salach

150 m

303m

SNH sp.

Glencripesdale

150 m

100 m

150 m

Glen Cripesdale

N

1 km

X

452m

See detail for the environs of Glencripesdale on the previous page.

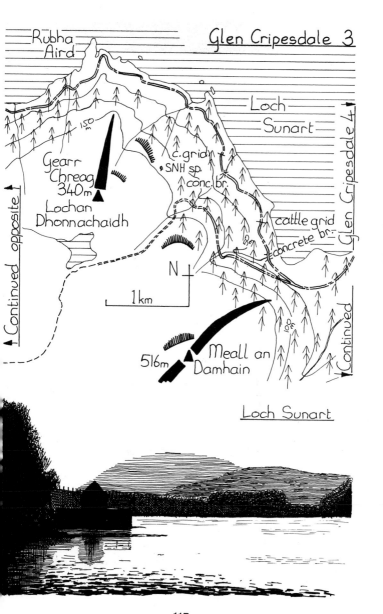

Rubha Aird

Loch Sunart

Gearr Chreag 340m

Lochan Dhonnachaidh

150m

c.grid
SNH sp.
conc. br.

cattle grid

concrete br.

N

1 km

Meall an Damhain

516m

Loch Sunart

◄ Continued opposite

Glen Cripesdale 4

Continued ►

Glen Cripesdale 4

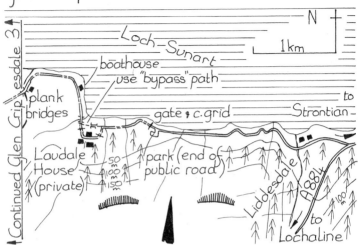

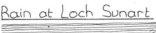

Rain at Loch Sunart

This route is not a glen - sorry! After a complex start, detailed below, the route becomes a grand traverse of the Point, high above the sea with a different view around every bend in the track. Views over Ardnamurchan are especially good. The far end of the track is a bit of an anti-climax, the return being back up a big hill. What a shame the track doesn't link up with Loch Teacuis at Barr - so near yet so far! The route boasts old mileposts indicating past importance. Suitable as a half day or short day's cycle or a full day walk the route is 11 km or 7 miles each way to the cottage, Doirlinn. An out-and-back route this leaves distance to choice. There is shelter as indicated. The start is at Bonnavoulin some (very pleasant) 18km or 11·5mls. north west of Lochaline.

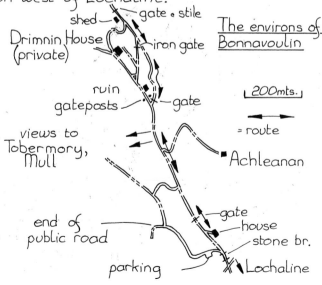

The environs of
Bonnavoulin

shed — gate & stile

Drimnin House
(private) — iron gate

ruin
gateposts — gate

200mts.

= route

views to
Tobermory,
Mull

Achleanan

end of
public road

gate
house
stone br.

parking

Lochaline

119

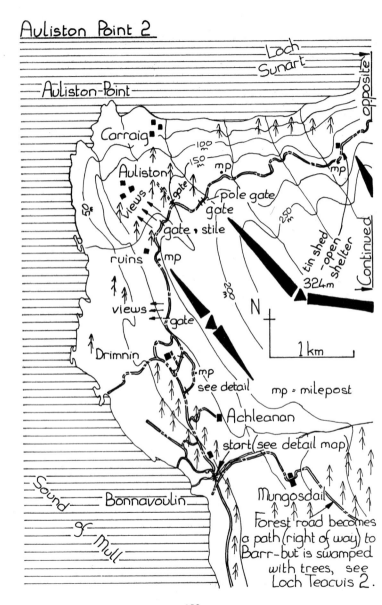

Loch Sunart

Auliston Point

opposite

Carraig

100

150

mp

mp

Auliston

views

gate

pole gate

gate

250 m

gate, stile

ruins

mp

tin shed
-open shelter

324m

Continued

200

views

300

gate

N

1 km

Drimnin

mp

see detail

mp = milepost

Achleanan

start (see detail map)

Sound

Bonnavoulin

Mungosdail

of

Mull

Forest road becomes
a path (right of way) to
Barr-but is swamped
with trees, see
Loch Teacuis 2.

120

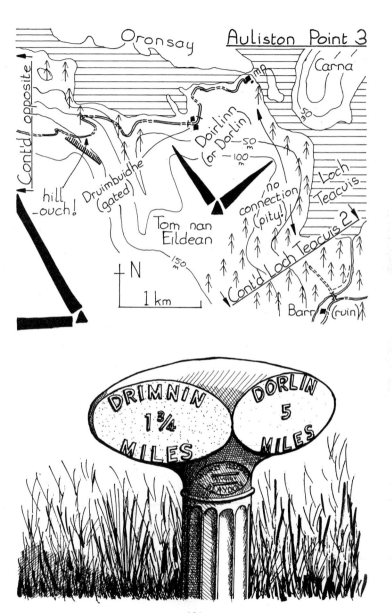

Oronsay

Carna

Contd// opposite

Doirlinn (or Dorlin)

hill -ouch!

Druimbuidhe (gated)

no connection (pity!)

Loch Teacuis

Tom nan Eildean

Cont'd Loch Teacuis 2

N

1 km

Barr (ruin)

DRIMNIN 1¾ MILES

DORLIN 5 MILES

Gleann Dubh 1

Gleann Dubh runs from north east to south west almost parallel with the A884, a few miles north of Lochaline. Indeed, why the A884 follows the present course involving a long climb to over 200m is a mystery for Gleann Dubh follows a much more obvious line. That said the 'A' road contours around the head of the glen giving fine views. [My wife and I remember this hill well as it was tackled "the morning after" a 90 mile ride around the coast of Mull - on a tandem! Our legs wouldn't work properly!] Gleann Dubh is best explored as a point-to-point walk; or as a short bike ride (from Acharn); or as a short walk taking in the picturesque gorge and woods. The one-way total distance is 11km or 7miles. There is no shelter.

<u>Gleann Dubh</u>

Gleann Dubh 2

Crosben

ruin –
Gleann Dubh

sign at
Acharn

RAHOY HILLS

WILDLIFE RESERVE

THE SCOTTISH WILDLIFE TRUST

Gleann Dubh 3

The start is adjacent to Acharn - amid a confusion of bits of old, abandoned road and bridges.

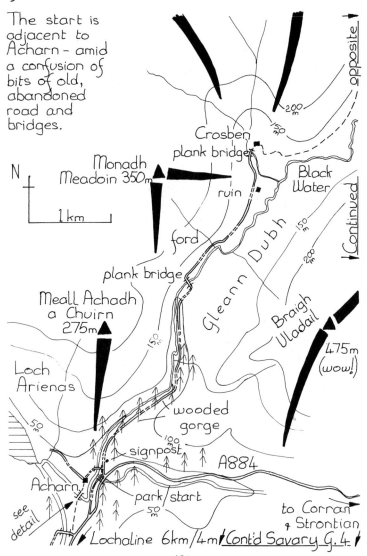

N

1 km

Monadh Meadoin 350m

Crosben
plank bridge

Black Water

ruin

Gleann Dubh

ford

150m

200m

plank bridge

Meall Achadh a Chuirn 275m

150

Braigh Uladail

475m (wow!)

Loch Arienas

50m

wooded gorge

100

signpost

A884

Acharn

see detail

park/start

50m

to Corran & Strontian

Lochaline 6km/4m

Cont'd Savary G.4

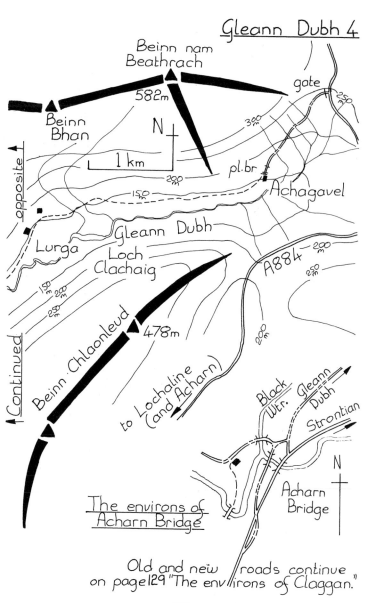

Beinn nam
Beathrach

582m

gate

Beinn
Bhan

300m

250

N

1 km

200

pl.br

150

Achagavel

opposite

Gleann Dubh

Lurga

Loch
Clachaig

A884

200m

150m 200m
250m

250m

200

Beinn Chlaonleud

478m

Continued

to Lochaline (and Acharn)

Black Wtr.

Gleann Dubh

Strontian

Acharn
Bridge

The environs of
Acharn Bridge

N

Old and new roads continue
on page 129 "The environs of Claggan."

125

Loch Teacuis 1

The exploration of Loch Teacuis and the Barr River is best done by bike. However the off-road section alone is too short so a start can be made from Loch Arienas to include the deserted public road which links this route into the Savary Glen forest tracks. Loch Teacuis is nearly much more: There is almost a way through to Dorlin, and Auliston Point; a walkers path strikes north to Glen Cripesdale only to be obliterated by forestry operations at its northern end; and a path leads south from Barr to Bonnavoulin, also sadly overgrown. Would the tree-planters please have a little respect for these old paths, many of which are rights of way? Is anyone out there listening? OK, sorry I shouted, but I feel a lot better with that off my chest! It had to be said ...... The ruin at Barr is spooky- but perhaps this is just your author being a wimp! The escarpment of Aoineadh Mor and Aoineadh Beag is worthy of note. There is no shelter. Approximate distances are as below:-

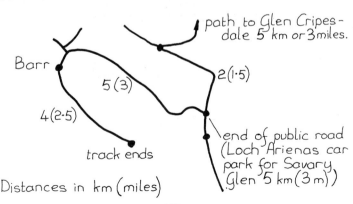

path to Glen Cripesdale 5 km or 3 miles.

Barr

5 (3)

2 (1·5)

4 (2·5)

track ends

end of public road (Loch Arienas car park for Savary Glen 5 km (3 m))

Distances in km (miles)

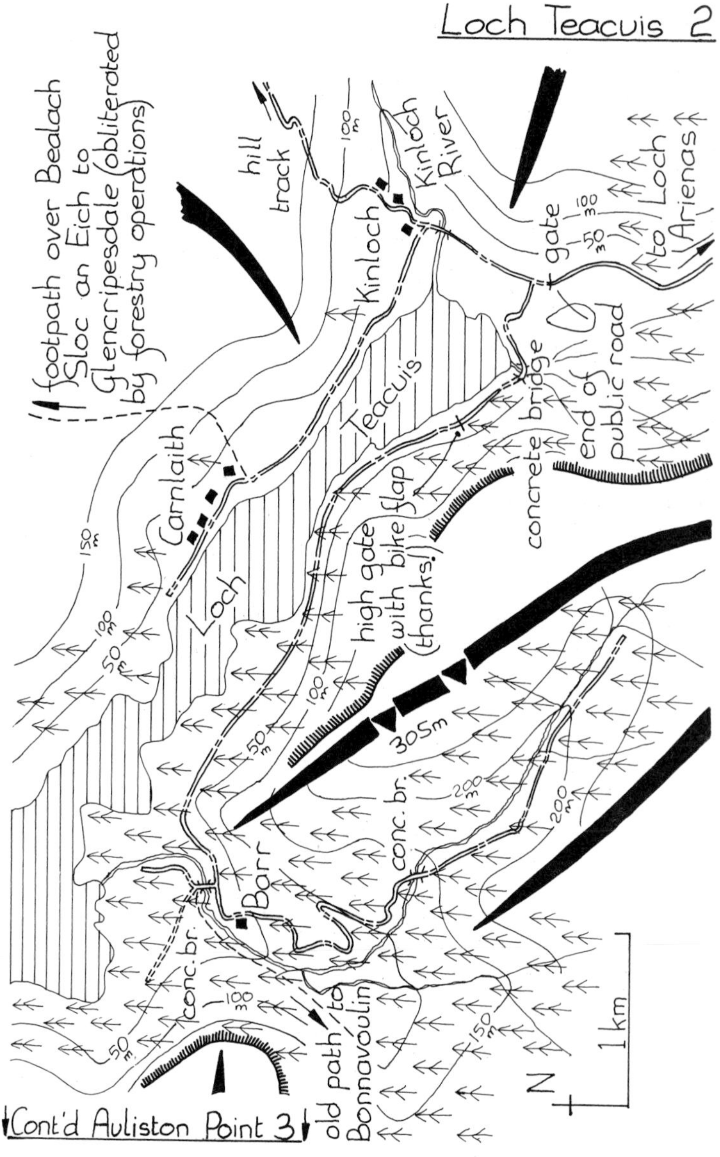

footpath over Bealach Sloc an Eich to Glencripesdale (obliterated by forestry operations)

hill track

100 m

Kinloch River

Kinloch

gate

100
50
30

to Loch Arienas

Kinloch

Teacuis

concrete bridge

end of public road

Carnlaith

150

100

50

Loch

high gate with bike flap (thanks!)

100 m

50 m

305 m

conc. br.

200
300

200

Barr

conc. br.

100
30

50 m

old path to Bonnavoulin

150

N

1 km

Cont'd Auliston Point 3

127

Savary Glen 1

Savary Glen and the surrounding forest tracks form an excellent mountainbike circuit (walkers would find the tracks tedious), but only if undertaken in a generally anti-clockwise direction as described below. Savary Glen itself is overgrown and grassy making its uphill passage extremely hard work and its downhill passage plain good fun, if a little 'technical'. The best starting point is Loch Arienas car park from which a steady climb south, then east, then south again, then west, then north (!) winds up to the head of Savary Glen. The track seems a bit endless at times but stay with it. The run down Savary Glen is very rough at the start but it does get better, and more fun, arriving eventually at the public road. (You will realise this track is difficult to find in the reverse direction as well as being hard work!) There are several options on the way back and for the purist the 'A' road can be avoided. Note track X-X can be used if the circuit is taken from Lochaline—in which village the hotel bar provides the only (very agreeable) shelter.

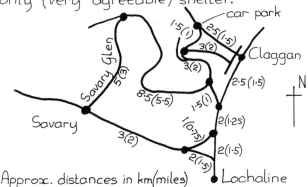

Approx. distances in km(miles)

128

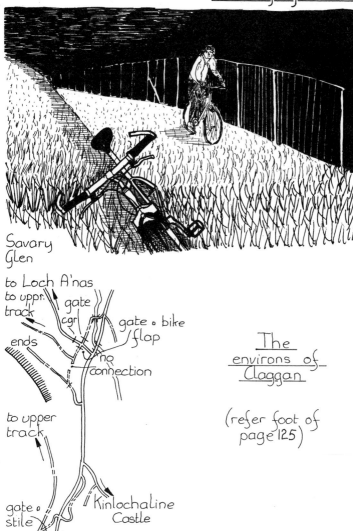

Savary
Glen

to Loch A'nas
to uppr.
track   gate
          cgr   gate o bike
                         /flap
ends
                    no
                 connection

to upper
track

gate o   Kinlochaline
stile   Castle

to Lochaline

The
environs of
Claggan

(refer foot of
page 125)

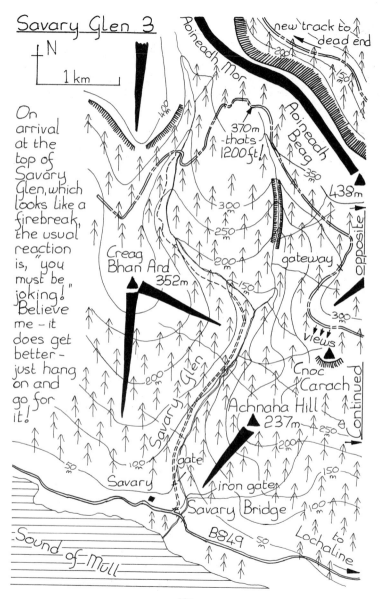

Savary Glen 3

N
1 km

On arrival at the top of Savary Glen, which looks like a firebreak, the usual reaction is, "you must be joking!" Believe me – it does get better – just hang on and go for it!

Aoineadh Mòr

new track to dead end
200
150

370m – thats 1200ft!

Aoineadh Beag

350

438m

300

250m

Creag Bhan Ard
352m

200m

150

gateway

300

views

Cnoc Carach

Achnaha Hill
237m

250m

200m

Savary Glen

200m

50m

100m

gate

Savary

iron gate

150m

250m

Savary Bridge

B849

50

100m

to Lochaline

Sound of Mull

opposite

Continued

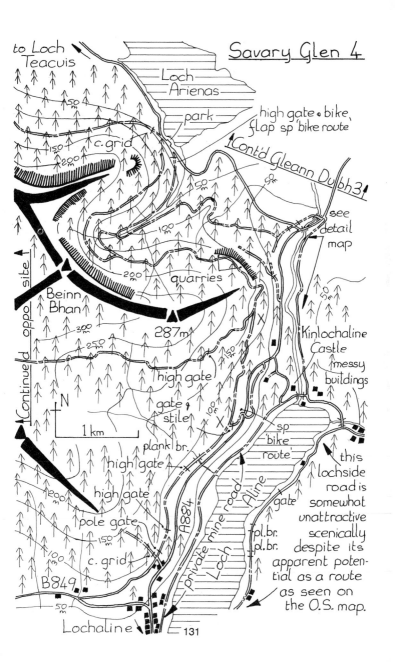

to Loch Teacuis

Loch Arienas

park

high gate . bike flap sp 'bike route'

Cont'd Gleann Dubh 31

c. grid

50m
150m
200m
100m
200m
300m
250m
50m

quarries

see detail map

Beinn Bhan

287m

Kinlochaline Castle

messy buildings

high gate

gate & stile

N
1 km

plank br.

sp 'bike route'

high gate

Aline

gate

high gate

pole gate

c. grid

A884

private mine road

Loch Aline

pl.br.
pl.br.

this lochside road is somewhat unattractive scenically despite its apparent potential as a route as seen on the O.S. map.

Continued opposite

200m
150m
100m
50m

B849

Lochaline

Link Routes

The link routes shown demonstrate how long through routes are made up from the various page maps. Variations can be planned using further adjacent routes but these should provide a basis for extended exploration.

The South Glenshiel Circuit

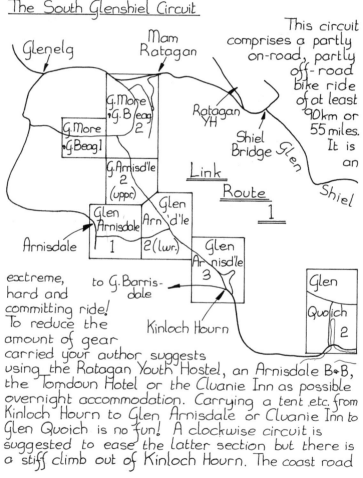

This circuit comprises a partly on-road, partly off-road bike ride of at least 90km or 55 miles. It is an extreme, hard and committing ride!

To reduce the amount of gear carried your author suggests using the Ratagan Youth Hostel, an Arnisdale B&B, the Tomdoun Hotel or the Cluanie Inn as possible overnight accommodation. Carrying a tent etc. from Kinloch Hourn to Glen Arnisdale or Cluanie Inn to Glen Quoich is no fun! A clockwise circuit is suggested to ease the latter section but there is a stiff climb out of Kinloch Hourn. The coast road

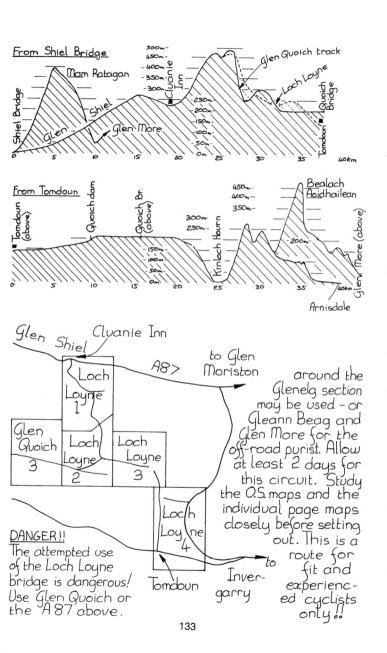

around the Glenelg section may be used – or Gleann Beag and Glen More for the off-road purist. Allow at least 2 days for this circuit. Study the O.S. maps and the individual page maps closely before setting out. This is a route for fit and experienced cyclists only!!

DANGER!!
The attempted use of the Loch Loyne bridge is dangerous! Use Glen Quoich or the A87 above.

Glenfinnan · Glen Kingie to Inverie

Link Route 2

Walkers' routes into Inverie, 'capital' of Knoydart, with starting points at Kingie and Quoich dam for the Glen Kingie approach;

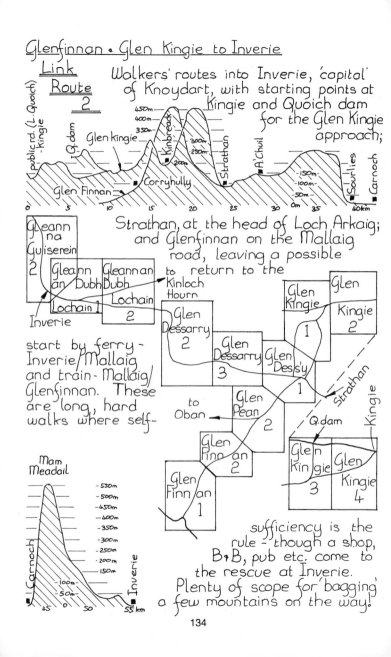

Strathan, at the head of Loch Arkaig; and Glenfinnan on the Mallaig road, leaving a possible to return to the start by ferry - Inverie/Mallaig and train - Mallaig/Glenfinnan. These are long, hard walks where self-sufficiency is the rule - though a shop, B&B, pub etc. come to the rescue at Inverie. Plenty of scope for 'bagging' a few mountains on the way!

134

The Kinloch Hourn approach to Knoydart

This is the most frequented route into Knoydart. It is the only route that connects the "mainland" roads to Inverie by way of an easily achievable single day's walk. This is not a bike route but the path is well engineered providing easy walking (for the west coast of Scotland that is!) throughout. There is a campsite and over-used bothy at Barrisdale Bay. The road loop to the west is worth walking for the coastal views. This has to be one of the most pleasant stretches of metalled road one can walk on - anywhere!

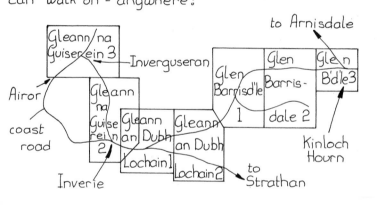

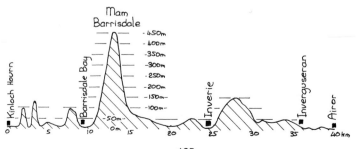

The Loch Shiel Circuit

This long circuit of about 73km or 46 miles is unfortunately not feasible by bike due to a) a rough path out of the head of Cona Glen; b) ditto between Glen Hurich and Glen Scaddle and c) a ban on cycles in Cona and Scaddle. However, despite the long plod along Loch Shiel it is worth doing on foot, with the odd day or three spent exploring some of the fine hills

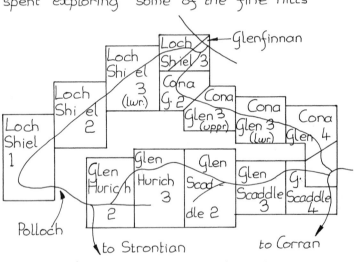

Glenfinnan

Loch Shiel 3

Loch Shiel 3 (lwr.)

Cona G. 2

Cona

Cona

Cona Glen 4

Glen 3 (uppr)

Glen 3 (lwr.)

Loch Shiel 2

Loch Shiel 1

Glen Hurich 2

Glen Hurich 3

Glen Scaddle 2

Glen Scaddle 3

G. Scaddle 4

Polloch

to Strontian

to Corran

around the head of glens Hurich, Scaddle and Cona. Loch Shiel is of course OK on a bike and may be used as a direct line between Glenfinnan and Strontian on the excellent forest track, not forgetting _that_ hill between Polloch and Strontian.

Gradient profile opposite ↗

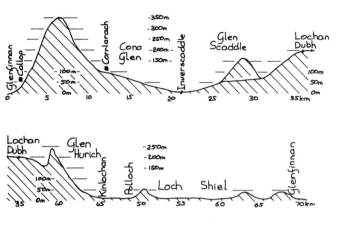

Note:-

It is worth noting that Link Route 1 is joined to Route 3 at Kinloch Hourn and Route 3 is in turn joined to Route 2 at Inverie Route 2 is tied into Route 4 at Glenfinnan, whilst Routes 1 and 2 are not a million miles apart at Tomdoun/Kingie/Quoich bridge. Great care is needed when planning longer excursions due to cycles being banned or discouraged, or the unsuitability of the path. Consult the detailed page maps and the O.S. maps for more detail. Be especially careful in Knoydart - it's special.

The research for Book 8 has probably been the most varied yet. Each previous area/book has had its own character but Book 8 encompasses such a variety of both scenery and walking or cycling terrain that if an award were due Book 8 would be the clear winner. There is true wilderness - my favourite type of country - long glens, wild camps and long days among the hills. The Rough Bounds of Knoydart fall into this category as, less obviously, does the head of Glen Scaddle and Cona Glen. There are long walkers' glens and short walkers' glens. Long bike rides; and short bike rides suitable for a half day or evening (most of these lie north of the Fort William to Mallaig road). Loch Garry provides a variety of tracks giving safe traffic-free family cycling with no big hills. Much of the charm, and excitement, of the area lies in its complex geographical forms with long glens, long fjord-like sea lochs (and long fresh water lochs!) and few roads. The area can only be touched upon with the motor car - for all its alleged convenience. To enjoy and appreciate the area fully the car has to be discard-ed (sorry about the pun - I'm trying to think deeply here - believe it or not!!) and bike, boots, tent and rucksack provide the means to escape the rat-race. Regular readers will know your author and his wife escaped the rat-race several years ago. If, dear reader you cannot or simply don't want to make your permanent escape then perhaps this series of books will provide the means or the incentive to escape for a day or a

week or longer. But escape we must to provide contrast between our work-a-day lives, however fulfilling, and the peace and tranquillity of the hills and glens.....

As I write this, research "work" for Book 9 is well advanced. The book will cover an area north of Glen Shiel, Glen Moriston and Loch Ness. Book 9 covers our 'back garden' and what a garden that is! Again an area of great variety - from west coast wilderness to eastern forest all set amid fine mountains separated by beautiful glens. It is intended, at present, that Book 9 will be the last in the series; the area to the north - Caithness and Sutherland - does not fall comfortably into the "glen" theme, and, frankly, there aren't enough visitors (or residents!) to justify a Book 10. I do not look forward to the anti-climax of completing the series. Your author will not, however be laying his pen to rest - so watch this space! I'll "see" you in Book 9.

CICERONE PRESS BOOKS ON SCOTLAND

WALKING IN THE ISLE OF ARRAN *Paddy Dillon* 41 day walks in this 'Scotland in Miniature'. *ISBN 1 85284 269 5 200pp £10.99*

THE BORDER COUNTRY - A Walker's Guide *Alan Hall* 53 walks in the Border Hills and Southern Uplands. *ISBN 1 85284 116 8 232pp £7.99*

BORDER PUBS & INNS - A WALKER'S GUIDE *Alan Hall* 53 pubs and inns with complete details of food, beers, access for children etc. and a suitable short walk based on each. *ISBN 1 85284 172 9 168pp £5.99*

THE CENTRAL HIGHLANDS 6 LONG DISTANCE WALKS *P.D.Koch-Osborne* Classic backpacking routes. *ISBN 1 85284 267 9 200pp £9.99*

CAIRNGORMS Winter Climbs *Allen Fyffe* Covers the best winter climbs in the Cairngorms, Lochnagar and Creag Meaghaidh. *ISBN 0 902363 99 9 120pp PVC cover £7.99*

WALKING THE GALLOWAY HILLS *Paddy Dillon* The wilderness hills of Galloway in southern Scotland. *ISBN 1 85284 168 0 168pp £7.99*

WALKING IN THE HEBRIDES *Roger Redfern* General descriptions and suggestions for walking routes in these varied, delectable Western Isles. *ISBN 1 85284 263 6 184pp £9.99*

WALKS IN THE LAMMERMUIRS, with Moorfoots, Broughton Heights and Culter Hills *Alan Hall* The lonely, stimulating hills between the River Tweed and Edinburgh. *ISBN 1 85284 214 8 216pp £9.99*

WALKING IN THE LOWTHER HILLS also Carsphairn Hills, the hills of Solway Coast, Tinto, and Cauldcleugh Head *Ronald Turnbull* Completes the Cicerone coverage of walking in Southern Scotland's hills *ISBN 1 85284 275 X 184pp £8.99*

NORTH TO THE CAPE *Denis Brooke & Phil Hinchliffe* A new walk from Fort William to the North Cape described in the authors' inimitable way with masses of maps and drawings. This will become a collector's item. *ISBN 1 85284 285 7*

THE ISLAND OF RHUM - A Guide for Walkers, Climbers and Visitors *Hamish M.Brown* The complete companion for any visitor to the island, owned by the Nature Conservancy. *ISBN 1 85284 002 1 100pp £5.99*

THE ISLE OF SKYE - A Walker's Guide *Terry Marsh* Walks in all parts of the island, from simple outings to rugged days in isolated situations, yet without scrambling. *ISBN 1 85284 220 2 216pp £9.99*

THE SCOTTISH GLENS *P.D.Koch-Osborne* *£5.99 each*

Book 1: CAIRNGORM GLENS *ISBN 1 85284 086 2 128pp*
Book 2: THE ATHOLL GLENS *ISBN 1 85284 121 4 144pp*
Book 3: THE GLENS OF RANNOCH *ISBN 1 85284 170 2 144pp*
Book 4: THE GLENS OF TROSSACH *ISBN 1 85284 199 0 144pp*
Book 5: THE GLENS OF ARGYLL *ISBN 1 85284 226 1 144pp*
Book 6: THE GREAT GLEN *ISBN 1 85284 236 9 144pp*
Book 7: THE ANGUS GLENS *ISBN 1 85284 248 2 144pp*
Book 8: KNOYDART TO MORVERN *ISBN 1 85284 282 2 144pp*
 The popular series of guides for walkers and mountainbikers.

SCOTTISH RAILWAY WALKS *H.M.Ellison* All the old lines are walked and nostalgically remembered. *ISBN 1 85284 007 2 192pp £6.99*

SCRAMBLES IN LOCHABER *Noel Williams* Some of the best scrambling in Britain around Glencoe and Ben Nevis and much of the Western Highlands too. *ISBN 1 85284 234 2 192pp £9.99*

SCRAMBLES IN SKYE *J.W.Parker* The Cuillins is a paradise for scrambling. *ISBN 0 902363 38 7 144pp PVC cover £7.99*

SKI TOURING IN SCOTLAND *Angela Oakley* 51 great ski-tours in all parts of the Highlands. *ISBN 1 85284 054 4 208pp £6.99*

TORRIDON - A Walker's Guide *Peter Barton* A comprehensive guide to this wild but beautiful area. *ISBN 1 85284 022 6 168pp £5.99*

WALKS from the WEST HIGHLAND RAILWAY *Chris & John Harvey* 40 walks, linear between stations or circular, based on a day's return travel from Glasgow. *ISBN 1 85284 169 9 £6.99*

THE WEST HIGHLAND WAY *Terry Marsh* A practical guide to this very popular walk. *ISBN 1 85284 235 0 112pp £6.99*

WINTER CLIMBS BEN NEVIS & GLENCOE *Alan Kimber* Britain's finest winter climbing area. *ISBN 1 85284 179 6 232pp PVC cover £14.99*

CICERONE PRESS produces a wide range of guide books covering much of Britain, Europe and other countries worldwide. Send s.a.e. for full catalogue and price list to:

CICERONE PRESS, 2 Police Square, Milnthorpe, Cumbria, LA7 7PU
Tel: 015395 62069 Fax: 015395 63417 E-mail:
info@cicerone.demon.co.uk

PRINTED BY CARNMOR PRINT & DESIGN, LONDON ROAD, PRESTON, LANCASHIRE